Hardy
COUNTRY

Hardy
COUNTRY

Tom Howard

CAXTON EDITIONS

PHOTOGRAPHIC ACKNOWLEDGEMENTS

Jacket front cover main picture:
A.F. Kersting
Jacket front cover black and white insets:
Hulton Deutsch Collection
Jacket back cover:
Derek Forss Photography

Inside pages
Brooke Photographic
14, 38, 47, 49, 51, 52 left, 53, 71, 78

Comstock Photo Library
10-11, 17, 18, 21, 29, 39, 41 bottom, 42, 44, 45, 55, 58-59, 63, 64, 70,
72 top, 73, 75 both, 77 bottom

Dorset County Museum
33

Edifice
28, 43

Derek Forss Photography
7, 37, 46, 50 top, 61 top, 66

Fortean Picture Library
31, 40 both, 41 top, 50 bottom

Jarrolds Publishing
57, 80

A.F. Kersting
2-3, 4-5, 12-13, 19, 20, 22, 24, 26, 27, 30, 32, 34-35, 48, 56, 60, 61,
bottom, 62, 67 top, 68, 69, 72 bottom, 74, 76, 77 top, 79 both

Clare Pawley 15, 45, 58, bottom (NB not open to the public), 59 bottom,
65, 67,

Viewpoint Projects
52 right, 54 all

Malcolm Porter
Map on pages 8-9

Clare Pawley would like to thank; Mr & Mrs C Edwards.

**Pages 2-3: Looking over Batcombe,
from Batcombe Hill, Dorset.
These pages: Eggardon Hill, near Powerstock.**

This Edition Published 2000 by
Caxton Editions an Imprint of
The Caxton Publishing Group

ISBN 1 84067 1130

Text copyright © 1995 Tom Howard
The right of Tom Howard of be identified as the author of this
work has been asserted by him in accordance with the Copyright,
Design and Patents Act, 1988

Copyright © 1995 Regency House Publishing Limited

Printed in Hong Kong.

CONTENTS

INTRODUCTION

Few writers can have drawn so directly on their own lives and background as Thomas Hardy did in his poems, novels and short stories. His sources are not only autobiographical, but drawn from earlier family history and local traditions for both plot and character: almost all his fictional topography is based on very real locations. Sometimes, well-known places and landmarks are actually named, more often they are given invented ones, their origins frequently recognizable from some similarity in form. If a particular setting is not readily identifiable, it is probably because it is a composite of more than one location. His fictional geography will sometimes stretch or shrink a distance or he will deliberately change a location to suit his story; but as he himself confirmed in the introduction to the 1912 Wessex Edition of his works, the landscape, antiquities and even the architecture which form the background to his novels is 'done from the real' – that is to say, it has some basis in reality, however elusive. In both his, and the reader's imagination the sense of place is extraordinarily powerful and his fiction has become as inseparable from the countryside in which it takes place as any real events that happened there.

The Wessex of Hardy's books exists only between his pages. But for those who wish to trace precise locations there have been numerous books which have set out to identify them for the reader. They had already begun to appear in 1902. In 1912, Hardy's friend, Hermann Lea (who was then living in the house where Hardy was born) produced *Thomas Hardy's Wessex*, and illustrated it with his own photographs. Hardy is supposed to have collaborated, though this may well have consisted more in not contradicting Lea's attributions than in confirming them. Denys Kay-Robinson's *The Landscape of Thomas Hardy* (1984) is a more recent and very detailed attempt and the Thomas Hardy Society publishes a series of pamphlets outlining tours to places linked with particular titles which may be ordered from them or from the County Museum in Dorchester.

This book aims at a much more general picture of the whole of Hardy Country for, fascinating though it may be to identify a particular building or village, it is the sense of the living countryside and country life that gives Hardy's writing its character rather than the accuracy of the topography.

Hardy was born in 1840, seven years before the railway reached Dorchester. He died in 1928, the year after Lindberg made his solo flight across the Atlantic. His own life bridged years of enormous social and technological change, but through his family and local memory he was able to reach back even beyond his childhood to the time of the Napoleonic Wars to embrace traditions which stretched back centuries earlier. He was accustomed to a world in which traditional folk magic was still practised, when public hangings still took place in Dorchester and was witness to the arrival in the marketplace of a horse-drill for sowing seeds, which was a source of amazement to labourers who for millennia had scattered seed by hand. In *Tess of the d'Urbervilles,* he describes a steam threshing-machine, typical of the innovations which were to change the pattern of agriculture in the following century. He saw the effects of the flooding of the market by the free trade in corn and other agricultural imports, and of the devastation wrought by bad harvests and disease. These inform his writing and, at the same time, celebrate the vitality of the rural tradition.

The real landscape in which Hardy's life and work was set still bears evidence of its historic past from the earliest settlements to Hardy's own time: despite the changes brought about by forestation, intensive agriculture and such modern intrusions as a nuclear power station, its downs and valleys still delight the eye with some of the loveliest scenery in southern Britain. Unlike Hardy, we do not have to capture these Wessex views in words but present them to you in fine photographs.

The statue of Thomas Hardy by Eric Kennington erected at Top 'O Town, Dorchester.

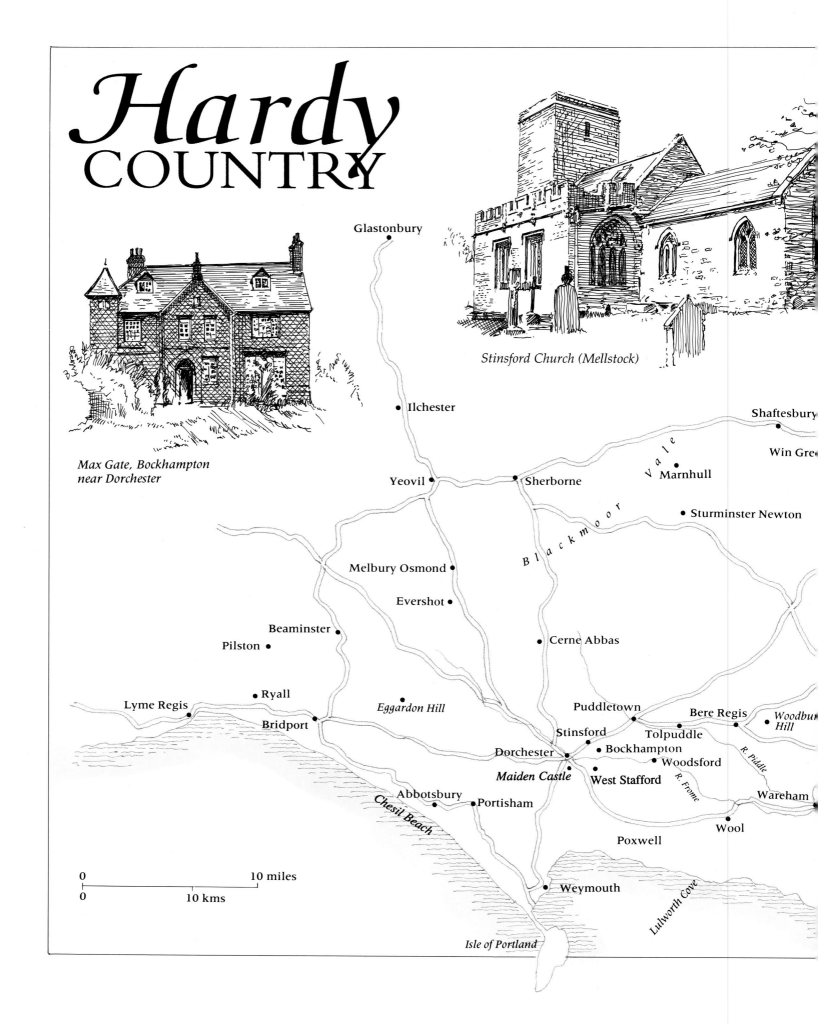

Hardy
COUNTRY

Max Gate, Bockhampton near Dorchester

Stinsford Church (Mellstock)

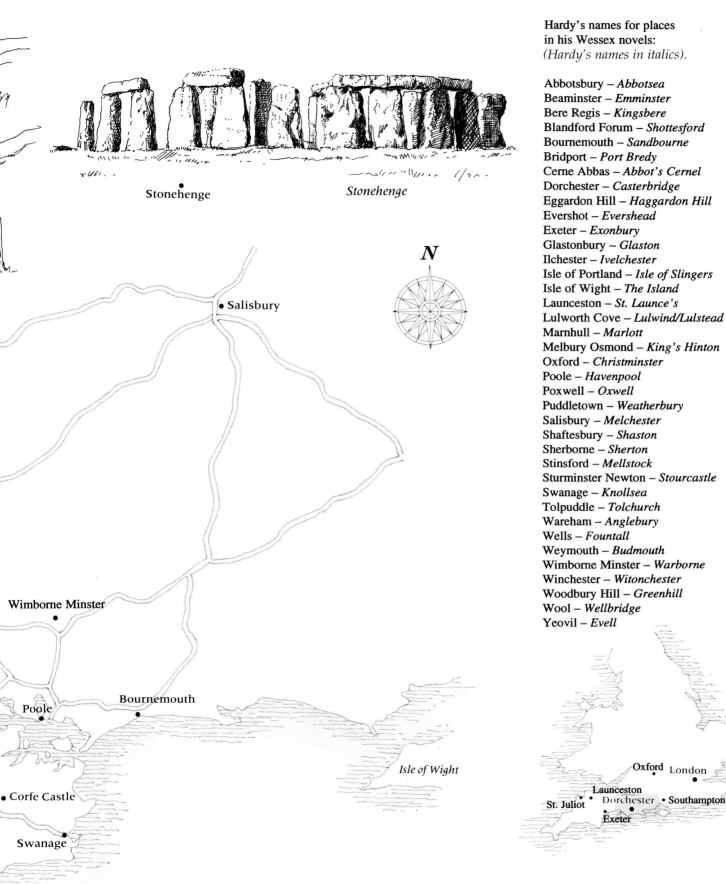

Stonehenge

Stonehenge

N

• Salisbury

Wimborne Minster

Poole

Bournemouth

Corfe Castle

Swanage

Isle of Wight

Oxford London

Launceston
St. Juliot Dorchester • Southampton
Exeter

Hardy's names for places in his Wessex novels:
(Hardy's names in italics).

Abbotsbury – *Abbotsea*
Beaminster – *Emminster*
Bere Regis – *Kingsbere*
Blandford Forum – *Shottesford*
Bournemouth – *Sandbourne*
Bridport – *Port Bredy*
Cerne Abbas – *Abbot's Cernel*
Dorchester – *Casterbridge*
Eggardon Hill – *Haggardon Hill*
Evershot – *Evershead*
Exeter – *Exonbury*
Glastonbury – *Glaston*
Ilchester – *Ivelchester*
Isle of Portland – *Isle of Slingers*
Isle of Wight – *The Island*
Launceston – *St. Launce's*
Lulworth Cove – *Lulwind/Lulstead Cove*
Marnhull – *Marlott*
Melbury Osmond – *King's Hinton*
Oxford – *Christminster*
Poole – *Havenpool*
Poxwell – *Oxwell*
Puddletown – *Weatherbury*
Salisbury – *Melchester*
Shaftesbury – *Shaston*
Sherborne – *Sherton*
Stinsford – *Mellstock*
Sturminster Newton – *Stourcastle*
Swanage – *Knollsea*
Tolpuddle – *Tolchurch*
Wareham – *Anglebury*
Wells – *Fountall*
Weymouth – *Budmouth*
Wimborne Minster – *Warborne*
Winchester – *Witonchester*
Woodbury Hill – *Greenhill*
Wool – *Wellbridge*
Yeovil – *Evell*

THOMAS HARDY: NOVELIST & POET

The Hardy family home at Upper Bockhampton, where Thomas Hardy was born in 1840. Although now faced with brick, his great-grandfather Thomas built the walls of cobb, the traditional mud wall, built up layer by layer with lime-wash with overhanging eaves to give protection from weathering. Originally there was probably only one room on each floor, the upper possibly curtained into several sleeping areas, the lower with a large fireplace. During Hardy's childhood his father either added the lower buildings at the south end or incorporated an existing barn. The cottage had 1¾ acres of land, enough to grow their own vegetables, have a pig, keep bees and grow cider apples in their own orchard. The house was used as a change-over point by smugglers bringing contraband up from the coast in his grandfather's day. It becomes the Dewys' home in *Under the Greenwood Tree* and among many poems Hardy wrote about his native district, *Domicilium*, his only one in blank verse is about this house.

Thomas Hardy was born on 2 June 1840 in the tiny hamlet of Higher Bockhampton about 4 km (2 ½ miles) from Dorchester, the county town of Dorset in southern England. His father and grandfather, who both bore the same name, and his great-grandfather John before them, were all builders by trade. However, young Thomas later preferred to dignify his father's trade with the name mason, and drew up a personal genealogy claiming descent from the Le Hardy family who were landowners on the island of Jersey in the English Channel. He also claimed kinship with the 16th-century Thomas Hardy who had founded Dorchester's

Grammar School and with the Admiral Thomas Hardy who was the captain of Horatio Nelson's flagship *Victory*. His immediate family were relatively humble, though rather more prosperous than the agricultural workers of the surrounding countryside.

Only 8km (5 miles) from Bockhampton is the village of Tolpuddle where, in 1833-4, only seven years before Thomas Hardy's birth, the 'Tolpuddle Martyrs' had been sent to a penal colony in Australia for attempting to form an agricultural union to improve their pitifully low wages. Over the years, cheaper imported foodstuffs and increasing mechanization of agri-culture led to further decline in rural prosperity and Hardy, as the picture of country life in his books confirms, would have been well aware of local conditions and the tenuousness of his higher status.

His mother, Jemima, though her maternal relations owned small pieces of land, came from an impoverished background. Her father seems to have drunk away much of the little he earned and her mother, disinherited by her family, who did not approve of the mar-riage, were forced to seek poor relief. Jemima went into service with the Earl of Ilchester and his relations, working for his uncle the Rector of Maiden

Newton and for the rest of the family when they went to London for the 'season'. She also worked for Ilchester's brother-in-law, the Vicar of Stinsford at Stinsford House. She had plenty of opportunity to observe the contrast between affluence and poverty and was determined that her children should avoid the deprivation experienced by their mother. She had known Thomas Hardy Senior for three years before her pregnancy hastened, if not forced their marriage: Thomas was born little more than five months after the ceremony in Melbury Osmond church. He may have been a little premature (though hardly by as much as three months) since the delivery was difficult and he was at first thought to be stillborn. It was the midwife who recognized signs of life and ensured his survival. Throughout his early years he was a sickly child whose survival to adulthood was always very much in doubt.

A year later a sister, Mary, was born to whom he became particularly close, and then after a ten-year gap a brother, Henry and in 1856 another sister, Katherine was born. Their father was a courteous, good-looking and easy-going man, popular in the community, a good dancer and fiddle player. But it was the more dominant Jemima who was to be the biggest influence in the children's lives.

Throughout his childhood, until her death when Thomas was 17, grandmother Hardy lived with the family in the bedroom next to the one he shared with his brother Henry. From her, he must have heard much of the past and history of the locality. His mother, too, possessed a rich store of local memories which she recounted to her children, at the same time hoping that their futures would be an improvement on the old days.

Though she was a lively and cheerful woman most of the time, it did not take much for her to fly into an angry mood and she could at times be intolerant and overbearing, especially after a miscarriage and subsequent illness a couple of years after Mary's birth.

Her children were brought up to be polite and well-spoken, protective of their own and with a strong sense of the importance of the family life. Jemima was not eager for them to marry and would have preferred them to live in

The bridge across the River Frome and the cottages of Lower Bockhampton. The first houses beyond the bridge were once a blacksmith's and alehouse which appear in Hardy's fiction.

brother and sister pairs, mutually supportive to one another. Careful with money, she encouraged them to keep what little they earned within the family. Thomas certainly inherited her streak of rural pessimism and clannishness. Her stronger influence ensured that he did not fall in with his father's more relaxed view of life, though as a boy he sometimes went out with his father to play with the village band and experienced the more ribald side of country life on such occasions.

The oral tradition of reminiscences and stories that Thomas absorbed when a very little child were to make a major contribution to his future writing: his mother was an avid and eclectic reader (her favourite book was said to be Dante's *Divine Comedy*) and Thomas also read voraciously long before he went to school. There was a dame school in Lower Bockhampton, but there is no evidence that he attended it. His uncertain health may have kept him at home, and his schooldays seem to have begun when he became the first pupil at the new parish 'National'

School (run by the church) when it was opened in 1848. It was endowed by the childless Julia Augusta Martin, wife of local landowner Francis Martin of Kingston Maurward house, who owned the land on which the Hardy house was built and whose estate provided much of the family's building work. Thomas was Mrs. Martin's particular favourite. He was greatly affected by the attention of this elegant and cultivated woman who inspired in him romantic and even erotic feelings which manifested themselves in poems written many decades later. As a young man he later attempted to re-establish a relationship, but recoiled with some shock at the clear evidence of a difference of more than 30 years in their ages.

In 1849, Hardy stayed for several months in Hatfield, north of London, where his mother went to help a sister through childbirth. On their return to Bockhampton it was decided to send him to school in Dorchester, causing a quarrel with Mrs. Martin which led to loss of work on the estate, though the building boom of the 1850s and '60s meant that his father's business was not seriously affected.

He was a year or more older than his classmates, though still small and looking younger than his ten years, but fit enough now to manage the daily walk of 4 km (2½ miles) into Dorchester again. When the headmaster, Isaac Last, left to establish an independent school for older pupils Hardy went with him. A serious student, well-liked by his fellow pupils, he took extra classes in Latin (and after he left school was able to teach himself Greek).

At 16, Thomas became an articled pupil in the office of Dorchester architect John Hicks. His mother required the usual premium for his instruction,

Fordington, with St. George's dominating the high ground, seen from the River Frome. This was still a noxious slum when Hardy was a boy. His uncle John lived there in Cuckold Row and he would pass close by on his daily walk into Dorchester on his way to school and later to John Hicks's office.

architectural drawing and surveying, being reduced to less than half. For three years he measured churches, made surveys, drew plans and copied drawings for the church 'restorations' and similar work that formed the main part of Hicks's business. His articles were extended for a year, not because of any incompetence on Thomas's part but because he was still felt to be too immature to seek other employment: when the time was up he joined Hicks's staff as a paid employee.

During this time, he became close friends with one of his workmates, Henry Bastow, a devout Baptist with whom he engaged in incessant religious discussion and who shared his interest in Latin and Greek. He made the acquaintance of William Barnes, another local schoolmaster and a dialect poet whose work he regarded highly, and of the sons of the Rev. Henry Moule of Fordington. Horatio (Horace) Moule, in particular, was to be an important influence in Hardy's life. Horace was a brilliant scholar who had been to both Oxford and Cambridge but failed to complete his degree at either. In Dorchester he was helping his father tutor private pupils. After episodes of alcoholism and possible misuse of opium he eventually committed suicide. This was before he had established himself as an essayist and book reviewer and Hardy considered that he had had the potential to be a major poet but for the fact that he had cut his own throat.

As for the opposite sex, young Hardy seems to have flirted with his own cousins with whom he was quite at ease. But his shyness, possibly attributable to the girl's higher social status, meant that his romantic attachment to the daughter of a local farmer remained a one-sided infatuation for he never even spoke to her.

At this time he seems to have been writing poems and some critical essays but he made no attempt to get them published.

In 1862, equipped with letters of introduction from Hicks, Hardy went to London to seek a post with a metropolitan architect. He found a place with Arthur Blomfield, whose large and fashionable practice was in offices just off Trafalgar Square, moving later to the Adelphi, overlooking the Thames. He took lodgings at 3 Clarence Place in Kilburn, which was then a leafy suburb, sharing with another young architect, moving the following year a few doors down the road and then to 16 Westbourne Park Villas, not far from

The National School which Thomas Hardy attended at Lower Bockhampton is now a private house, its appearance changed by modern windows But the old bell which called Thomas Hardy to school still hangs over the entrance porch.

the Paddington railway terminus.

Blomfield was pleased with his work, proposing him for membership of the Architectural Association. It was routine rather than onerous work. The staff would often sing together as they worked at their drawing desks and Hardy found time to write poetry in the office as well as in his lodgings. Most of his free hours were devoted to reading and study, guided by the advice of Horace Moule, but he found time to visit the theatre, attend a lecture by Dickens and to make occasional visits to restaurants with work colleagues and friends. He got to know a young woman called Eliza Nicholls who was in service a few streets away from his Paddington lodgings – indeed, it is possible that he may have known her already since some years earlier her father had been a coastguard at Kimmeridge Bay in Dorset. They appear to have considered themselves engaged to be married. She was obliged to leave London to nurse her employer's father and then returned to her family in Sussex. Separation does not seem to have made the heart grow fonder and on a visit to her home Hardy discovered that he had a much greater interest in her younger sister. Their 'engagement' came to an end in 1867, though Eliza still seems to have carried a torch for him for half a century more (after his first wife's death she visited him, apparently thinking her time had come at last). The experience was described at the time and later in several poems and stories.

In March 1864, *Chamber's Journal* accepted for publication an article on 'How I Built Myself a House' and Hardy begun to think of himself as a poet. He came to see ordination and a country curacy as an ideal way of life giving him security, respectability and enough spare time to pursue his literary ambitions. His classical studies were a good preparation and he made enquiries about entering Salisbury Theological College and, through the Moules, about trying to get into Cambridge – a degree in divinity being the entry qualification to Orders. However, even if he had been able to find the resources to support himself through the seven years at college, he possibly had not attained the standards required for university entrance and a realization of this together with the widening chasm between his own ideas and Anglican orthodoxy caused him to abandon these aspirations. This realization, the fact that none of the publishers to whom he had sent his poems showed any interest, the collapse of his relationship with Eliza and the indication that her sister preferred another man, all contributed to an increasing feeling of frustration. Throughout his life there were often to be periods when black, almost suicidal depression descended upon him. Compounded by lack of sleep from long hours of writing and study, his health became seriously undermined. An invitation to return to John Hicks's practice strengthened his decision to go back to Dorset.

Horace Moule suggested that Hardy might do some reviews in his spare time but this was not something that Hardy ever pursued. If he was unable to interest publishers in his poetry he decided he would try his hand at a novel. In 1867-8 he wrote *The Poor Man and the Lady*. No version of it survives but it appears to have been the story of a young peasant, who, like Hardy has become an architect who loves the squire's daughter. They are separated but eventually secretly marry, though the lady suddenly dies. The hero has radical reformist views and the novel sets out to satirize both country life and London society.

Moule recommended that the story be sent to the publishers, Macmillan's, whose reader found it promising. Alexander Macmillan responded with an encouraging letter saying that if this was a first novel he should keep on writing; he was interested enough to say that he was seeking other advice on what changes, as far as presentation of the upper classes were concerned, might make the book more acceptable. Later the manuscript was returned and Hardy attempted his own revisions before resubmitting it. He went to London to see Macmillan who suggested he try another publisher, Chapman and Hall who actually offered to publish the book if Hardy would guarantee them £20 against loss. However, they too later advised against publication without major changes and would have preferred a new and more

strongly plotted story. He tried other publishers, one of whom also offered publication for a premium against loss which Hardy considered too high: but the book was never published. Instead, elements of it were incorporated into his later fiction. In the latter part of 1869 he was at work on a new book, *Desperate Remedies*, with a sensational plot of murder and mystery which used earlier material from the rejected novel. Macmillan's found it too shocking but William Tinsley, who had been prepared to issue *The Poor Man and the Lady* said that, provided he made alterations, they would publish it for a guarantee of £75, terms which Hardy accepted in May 1870.

Meanwhile, there had been other developments in Hardy's life. Hicks had died and his practice was taken over by G.R. Crickmay, an architect

St. Juliot's Church, Cornwall, where Hardy was sent to work on 'restoration' of the church in 1870. This was to involve pulling down the old tower, north aisle and north transept and removing a rood-screen and old carved pews.

OPPOSITE

Inside St. Juliot's. The modern nave is the south aisle of the old church. Hardy later much regretted the scale of demolition, but the fabric was in a bad state and he claimed the decision to demolish had been made long before he was involved.

BELOW

The Valency valley at St. Juliot's, Cornwall. As 'West Endelstow' in *A Pair of Blue Eyes*, Hardy moved the village much closer to the coast.

based in Weymouth, on the coast south of Dorchester, and Hardy decided to move house there to help finish existing commissions. Then, after a break in Bockhampton he was sent to Cornwall to handle the repair of the church at St. Juliot, arriving to survey and measure the building on 7 March 1870.

St. Juliot is in the valley of the little River Valency which flows into the sea at Boscastle, not far from Tintagel. Living at the rectory with the Rev. Caddell Holder and his wife was her unmarried sister, Emma Gifford. It was she who greeted him on arrival – Mrs. Holder was busy nursing her husband who was in bed with gout. In the five days he was there he spent a great deal of time with him, taking him on walks about the district, playing the piano in the evenings and discussing literature

when she discovered he wrote poetry. It is hardly surprising that Hardy should have appeared more interesting than the local farmer whom she had it in her sights to marry, and she impressed him with her long, corn-coloured ringlets, naive charm, her middle-class gentility distinguishing her from the farm girls and maidservants Hardy had previously known. He was approaching 30 and looked older; Emma, though close to six months less, looked much younger (and the following year falsified a census return by declaring herself to be only 25). Both she and her family seemed eager to get her a husband but by the time Hardy returned to Dorset he appears to have been thoroughly enchanted by her. In August (by which time he was working in London for Blomfield and another prominent architect called Raphael Randon) he

returned to Cornwall for three weeks. The poem, 'The Place on the Map' set in the long hot summer of 1870, rather suggests that his relationship with Emma had become sexually intimate leading Hardy to feel honour-bound to marry her; but he appeared to have considered himself engaged when he returned to Bockhampton. There were four more years of letters and meetings in Cornwall and Bath before their wedding day.

Hardy revised *Desperate Remedies,* sending the manuscript to Emma to make a clean copy, and Tinsley accepted it for publication on the agreed terms. It was published anonymously in three volumes in March 1871. The handling of its rustic characters was well received by critics but most found it coarse (a rape sets the plot in motion) and *The Spectator* was particularly savage. Stung by the reviews but encouraged by publication Hardy began another book drawing directly on his rural background, *Under the Greenwood Tree,* again salvaging scenes from the abandoned *The Poor Man and the Lady*, To earn a living, he went back to working for Crickmay in Weymouth, with weekends usually at Bockhampton, then to London to T. Roger Smith, professor at the Royal Institute of British Architects, with whom he was preparing designs for new schools in the capital.

The new novel was offered to Macmillan's who would not commit themselves and postponed making a decision until the spring. When Tinsley returned nearly £60 of his premium (more than he had been led to expect) he decided to let them have it for £30 outright, a decision he was later to

Boscastle Harbour
'Castle Boterel' where the Valency reaches the sea.

regret. It was published in June 1872 to good reviews but followed by poor sales. Nonetheless, Tinsley expressed an interest in a new book to be serialized in the monthly magazine they published. For *A Pair of Blue Eyes*, a fee was agreed of twice the amount Hardy could expect to earn as an architect in the nine months he had to write it, even though he only had the rights for the serialization and three-volume publication. He left his London job at the end of July and had the first installment to Tinsley by 7 August for publication a week later. He asked for proofs to be sent to Emma's father's house near Bodmin and from there he departed to St. Juliot. This novel draws on his Cornish experiences and courtship and on incidents recounted by Emma. She again became his copyist and later suggested that she had been co-author of much of Hardy's work, rather than his amanuensis.

In August, Smith asked him to undertake more architectural work but, with Emma's approval, he decided to devote himself entirely to writing. An extra payment from Tinsley of £10 – half the receipts from selling Continental rights in *Under the Greenwood Tree* and an invitation from Leslie Stephens (who had discovered the identify of that book's author from Horace Moule) to contribute a serial to his magazine came as reassuring support for that decision. Stephens (father of Virginia Woolf) was editor of the prestigious *Cornhill* and was not aware that Hardy was already writing a serial for *Tinsley's Magazine*. For him *Far from the Madding Crowd* was written, at Bockhampton, the story being set in the the close neighbourhood.

All Hardy's novels from now on appeared first in serial form. This caused problems; for the readership of the magazines which published them

Lanhydrock House, in the Fowey Valley, near Bodmin, a house which Hardy saw when he went to Cornwall to meet his father-in-law in 1872. It suggested 'Endelstow House' in *A Pair of Blue Eyes*.

was much more easily shocked and offended than those who bought novels in book form. Incidents such as the seduction of Fanny Robin by Sergeant Troy and the finding of her dead baby by Bathsheba was more than they could stomach – though this was toned down in *Cornhill* so that a servant simply whispers the information to Bathsheba leaving the reader to fill in the details. Although Hardy frequently assured his potential publishers that there would be nothing offensive or upsetting in the stories he planned to write, he frequently found himself stepping beyond what was appropriate for this market and was consequently forced to compromise and re-work material which he would then restore for later volume publication.

Far From the Madding Crowd proved popular in both serial and book form. Hardy was now firmly established and in September 1874, he and Emma were married at St. Peter's, Paddington, in London.

After a weekend in Brighton the Hardys went to Paris for their honeymoon (though Thomas wrote to his brother that he was going there to gather material for his next story). This was the first of a number of Continental expeditions which they made together: in 1876 they travelled to Rotterdam and through Germany to Cologne, Baden Baden, Strasbourg and Metz and then visited Brussels and the battlefield of Waterloo; in 1887 they went to Italy and visited Genoa, Florence, Rome and Venice; in 1896 to Belgium and the following year to Switzerland.

Back in London, they rented a recently-built house in Surbiton, a suburb some way out of London. St. David's Villa, Hook Road, was their first married home. It was a quarter of an hour's walk to the railway station, then the best part of a half-hour journey into central London, not the kind of fashionable background to which Emma aspired, nor an appropriate setting from which to launch a successful author on society. They stayed there less than six months, moving to a street not far from Hardy's former lodgings in North Kensington but, perhaps because of the expense of living in London and partly because Hardy found it difficult to write when living in the city, they decided to move back to Dorset. In July 1875, they took rooms in West End Cottage, on the hillside above the seaside town of Swanage. But by then he had another novel, *The Hand of Ethelberta* already appearing in *Cornhill*. In Swanage he continued to work on this story, which has a Wessex opening but is largely set in London.

Emma was not the kind of woman Hardy's mother would have liked him to have married and there was always a certain coolness between the two women. It was thought wise to keep some distance from Bockhampton, though Hardy's sisters did make some attempt to be friendly; initially at least. The following spring Thomas and Emma moved westward to Yeovil, in Somerset, and after a European holiday, to Sturminster Newton, northwest of Dorchester in the Vale of Blackmore. Here, fully mistress of her own home at last, Emma was more content and the couple began to make local friends. Two of her brothers came to stay and at Christmas Emma visited Bockhampton. It was in that area that he set the novel on which he was now working, *The Return of the Native*.

Leslie Stephens turned it down for *Cornhill*, considering it likely to prove 'too dangerous' for a family magazine, and it was eventually placed with Chatto and Windus's *Belgravia* for serialization and Smith, Elder (publishers of the Brontës) for book publication.

Before he had finished writing it they moved back to London to a house in Tooting, a suburb south of the Thames. Emma had aspirations towards self-advancement in social and literary circles, a goal she was unlikely to achieve at Sturminster. Sadly, it was a way of life to which she was ill-suited. As she grew older, the girlishness which had seemed so attractive in her youth began to pall. She certainly did not make a good impression on some of her husband's literary colleagues in the succeeding years. Hardy himself began to be more and more disillusioned with his marriage.

He now spent many hours in the reading room of the British Museum making notes for an historical novel *The Trumpet Major*, set in Napoleonic times. This was eventually placed with a

magazine called *Good Words,* and required a number of amendments to make its serialization acceptable for 'family readership'. Hardy, meanwhile, committed himself to a novel for a European edition of *Harper's New Monthly* Magazine: *A Laodicean,* to start serialization in December 1880. That autumn he was taken ill, suffered a haemorrhage and was told he must either undergo an operation or have a long period of rest with his feet higher than his head. Choosing the latter meant five months housebound with Emma and with monthly deadlines for the installments.

In June 1881, the Hardys moved back to Dorset, to Wimborne, where they stayed two years before taking a house in Dorchester, where Hardy now bought a plot of land on the Wareham road, east of the town. Here he built Max Gate, which was to be his home from June 1885 until his death. These years saw the completion of a novel for the *Atlantic Monthly*. It was called *Two on a Tower* and he researched the astronomical background and a systematic search through the files of the local newspaper to build up the Dorchester background which he used in *The Mayor of Casterbridge:* it was completed by the time they moved into the new house and began serialization in the *Graphic* in January 1886.

Max Gate was within easy reach of Bockhampton and Hardy saw a great deal of his family, though Emma kept her distance. There were occasional visitors but Hardy's life centred upon his work, retiring to his study to write for most of the day. Emma continued to assist, at least with copying or dictation, for some of the manuscript of *The Woodlanders* is in her hand; but their differences in outlook were widening and, rather than solving their problems, the new house seemed to intensify them.

The book was another reminder of the class division between them but, if Emma was conscious of marrying 'beneath' her, Hardy failed to find in her the companion in mind and spirit which he had first imagined. Like some of the literary critics she was not happy with the pessimism of his novels and the 'immorality' which seemed ever present, however much it might be toned down for the magazine readership.

The Woodlanders was completed at the beginning of February 1887 and, after spending the next few weeks making revisions for the volume edition, the Hardys set off for a tour of Italy. Hardy's writing became increasingly critical of marriage but the couple worked and stayed together. Hardy's patience impressed visitors and he showed great consideration towards Emma spending a great deal of time at home with her.

They returned from Italy to find *The Woodlanders* had been well received, took lodgings in Kensington and remained in London until late July. A member of the Savile Club, involved with the Society of Authors and a guest in literary salons, Hardy was able to freely move in the world of books and was making some close literary friends. Much as Emma benefited from the prestige and glamour which came from her husband's literary success she was unable to play any real part in that world.

For most of the 1880s and 1890s, the Hardys spent some time in London during the summer months. On his own Hardy frequently stayed in a temperance hotel but with Emma rented a house or apartment. The winter was devoted to writing.

In London, Emma enjoyed meeting well-known people, though it became increasing clear that she cut a very odd figure among them. For Hardy, as well as his literary friends, there were numerous opportunities to meet women within the social and literary worlds and Hardy made a number of attachments of a more or less romantic nature. Often he would leave Emma behind, even when they were both in London. Though there is no evidence of any sexual affairs, Emma did have reason for being jealous of his interest in other women: though she resented the attention he gave his family even more. Increasingly, in later years, Hardy would go alone to stay with friends or visit London.

Hardy contracted to write his next novel for Tillotson's, a company which syndicated serials to newspapers and magazines but first he wrote a number of short stories for magazines, some of them published together as *Wessex Tales*. It was not until the early autumn of 1889 that he began to concentrate on *Too Late Beloved* (later to become *Tess of the d'Urbervilles*), though he had been developing the story and his characters in the preceding months and had it almost half complete. Much of it had already been typeset when Tillotson's became alarmed at the way the story was going and, when Hardy refused to make sufficient changes, it was agreed to cancel the contract. After two magazines also rejected it he did set about some re-writing and took up an earlier invitation to write a serial for the *Graphic*. He did not send them the completed text but it was agreed he would complete half by September 1890 and the rest in installments. Meanwhile he wrote some short stories, *A Group of Noble Dames* for the *Graphic*. Again, after reading proofs, the publishers realized they would not be suitable for their family readership. They rejected two and insisted on extensive revisions to others. *Harper's*, the American publishers, were not so cautious and

accepted them without bowdlerization.

Hardy took his brother to France in August and was late in delivering the first half of *Tess*, but by the end of October the *Graphic* had the complete book – to which inevitably changes had to be made: two passages that were cut were published as a separate story in the less scrupulous *Fortnightly Review!* Adherence to 'family values' required that Tess was not seduced but put through a bogus wedding; that she did not have a child, and that she lived with Alec d'Urberville on purely platonic terms. In lesser matters too 'Mrs. Grundy' had to be satisfied: for instance, Angel Clare was not allowed to carry a dairymaid through the flood – he had to fetch a wheelbarrow for her to ride in! Even when first put into volume form, Tess's acquiescence to

LEFT
Max Gate, designed by Hardy himself, did not originally have the right-hand turret with the sundial.
The house was gradually expanded to accommodate their greater needs, especially as Thomas and Emma began to feel the need for their individual personal space. The house had no bathroom. Hot water for washing was carried up to the bedrooms by their maid.

ABOVE
Max Gate as seen from the garden.

seduction had to be justified by first drugging her with alcohol! These changes, however, did not prevent the novel from being a great success.

Tillotson's were promised that the next serial would contain nothing that could 'offend the most fastidious taste'. *The Pursuit of the Well-Beloved*, the story of a man falling in love with three look-alike generations, mother, daughter and

16 Pelham Crescent, in South Kensington. The Hardys took this London house for two separate summers. They rented many different houses and apartments for their visits to the city and never owned a London property.

granddaughter in succession, met with no problems.

In 1894, a collection of previously published stories, *Life's Little Ironies*, was well received and meanwhile, as the next novel for *Harpers*, Hardy promised 'a tale that could not offend the most fastidious maiden'. But as he wrote his story of 'a young man who could not go to Oxford' he realized that the sexual aspect of *Jude the Obscure* was going to cause problems and offered to cancel their agreement. They declined, but did insist on changes: in the serialization Jude does

not beget children, they become someone else's orphans.

In *Jude*, Hardy drew on his own frustrated aspirations which had denied him university and ordination, but he also poured into it his feelings about marriage: 'a sordid contract, based on material convenience'. The book was particularly important to him. As he wrote to a woman friend, he was 'more interested in this Sue story than in any I have written'. When issued in volume form, with the sexual elements more explicit, in November 1895, he was ill-prepared for the way in which it was attacked. The presentation of marriage, the brutalism of scenes such as the killing of a pig, and its bleakness, all drew critical condemnation.

It is surprising that, despite the comments of editors and critics of earlier work, Hardy should be so naive about the reactions his work would produce. However, he was not to risk their censure again: apart from some short stories, this was the last prose fiction he published. In future, he devoted himself almost exclusively to poetry (if the volumes of autobiography which he prepared for publication under the name of his second wife are excluded).

Poetry had always been Hardy's first love; he had devoted his energies to novels because he needed to support himself and Emma, but now he seemed assured of the comparatively small income they would need for the years they had left – he was already 56. Perhaps, also, he felt that his darker sentiments would find easier acceptance if they were expressed in verse.

Hardly any of Hardy's poetry had appeared in print but he had never stopped writing it. Now his fame and literary reputation would help to sell his verse (though he offered to pay the cost of producing the first volume himself). He made a selection of poems to form a volume which he called *Wessex Poems and Other Verses* and they were published with some of his own drawings at the end of 1898. The critics were puzzled and largely negative, they certainly did not admire them as people do today.

He was to publish a further six volumes of poetry and an epic drama in 19 acts dealing with Napoleon and his

sword, just as they had been in the 19th century B.C., seemed to Hardy to justify the most extreme pessimism. While he recognized the excitement which was generated and could celebrate martial themes in his writing he was an internationalist who abhorred war. When hostilities were over he expressed the belief that people would increasingly be able to understand other peoples'

Stinsford Church, where Jemima Hardy was buried in 1904. Her grave is the first on the right. So long as she was alive Hardy's ties to her and to his Bockhampton background were probably stronger than any other in his life. But since she did not approve of his marriage to Emma there was never any goodwill between the two women. Stinsford was Hardy's 'Mellstock'.

times: *The Dynasts* written in verse and prose. He had always been interested in the period and even before writing *The Trumpet Major* was thinking of a larger treatment – the first notes for an 'Iliad of Europe' were made in 1875. He was already researching the background before *Wessex Poems* was published but it was to be another five years before the first part appeared in print and 1908 before all three parts were published.

Within a year of the publication of *Wessex Poems* the Boer War began. The fact that at the end of the 19th century arguments were still being settled by the

points of view and war-making would come to an end. But that day – if it ever comes – was far away. Only 14 years later Europe became embroiled in the First World War. Hardy was one of a group of writers invited to show support for the British cause. He wrote a group of poems to endorse the need to stand firm against aggression – Hardy gave no support to outright pacifists – while expressing his compassion for the ordinary people involved. Nearly two years before the Great War was unleashed, Emma Hardy died. There were many things that they had shared,

Larmer Tree Gardens at Rushmore, on the Dorset-Wiltshire border, entertainment grounds created by the archaeologist, General Augustus Pitt-Rivers. Here Hardy met the general's daughter Agnes Grove in 1885 and danced with her with such abandon that onlookers wondered whether they were intoxicated. This is said to be the last time Hardy danced and his admiration for Agnes and the encouragement he gave her writing, along with similar attentions to other ladies, did not help to relieve the tensions in his marriage.

including a love of animals. As late as 1895, when both were in their mid-50s, Hardy had learned to bicycle so that he could accompany Emma who had already taken up the new fashion; but though they still dined and entertained together, their lives were becoming increasingly separate. Emma made trips to London, Brighton, even to Calais without him and had taken over two rooms as her own, one as her bedroom, the other as a study where she worked on her own poems and stories. She resented the fact that the contribution she felt she had made to Hardy's earlier work was never acknowledged and that she was no longer a part of his writing. Being his wife sometimes helped get her publication, but Hardy made no attempt to help or promote her though he made efforts to encourage certain others of

the female sex. He wrote poems about other women rather than her, and she was upset by what she saw as criticism of marriage in his work.

As the century progressed, Emma was troubled by ill-health. She had a seizure of some kind in 1906, possibly followed by other 'fainting fits' which stopped her from cycling until 1910, but otherwise no major problems. However, by 1912, when the Hardys were into their 70s, she was often too frail to walk to church and was pushed there in a Bath chair. In November she had severe back pain and was unable to face food, but refused to call a doctor, though one did come the next day. The following morning her maid, coming up to wake her, found her moaning with pain. On Emma's instruction she fetched Hardy but by the time he arrived she was unable to

speak and minutes later died. Less than 14 months later he remarried.

Hardy's second wife was Florence Dugdale, whom he had met in 1905. How, is unclear: Florence later told several versions, one being of the time she was a 26-year-old schoolteacher, dissatisfied with her job and looking for literary work. She became one of the women Hardy helped, and she in turn helped him, looking up references and historical background for *The Dynasts* and later typing his manuscripts. On one occasion when it was thought that Emma might come up to London it was arranged that Hardy's friend Edward Clodd should accompany Florence to the opera and that Hardy would see her in the interval. Later there were visits together to Clodd's house at Aldeburgh on the Suffolk coast. She met Emma at the Lyceum Club (a women's literary club) and after coming to her assistance when she muddled the notes for a speech she was making, was invited to one of Emma's London 'at homes'. Soon she was generally assisting Emma, giving the older woman support and encouragement in her literary efforts. By 1910 she was frequently at Max Gate but after a blazing row when Hardy expressed a wish to take Florence to visit his sisters on Christmas Day, where Emma was convinced they would try to turn Florence against her, she avoided being there when both Hardys were at home.

There is no evidence of any physical infidelity on Hardy's part but, though Florence was 38 years his junior, she was very like him in temperament and the attachment was very strong. Her

Tintagel, a medieval castle on a rocky promontory which has long been associated with King Arthur, though there is probably no historical connection. Hardy returned here with his brother when retracing the excursions he had made with Emma.

The Hardy family graves in Stinsford churchyard. Thomas Hardy's heart is buried in the same grave as Emma. Jemima and his father are buried on the right and the adjoining upright stones mark the graves of his grandfather, grandmother, uncle and cousins.

admiration of his work was in contrast to Emma's later disapproval and she was a willing helpmate. This was also largely how she saw herself when she became his wife. There are some hints that she may have been sexually reticent and it has been said that Hardy was impotent, though in his old age he reportedly still claimed to be capable of sexual intercourse until he was 84.

However unsatisfactory their marriage had been, Emma's death hit Hardy hard and when he discovered and read her diaries he was flooded with memories of the young Emma and his feelings for her. In the spring of 1913 he made a nostalgic return to Cornwall and the places where their romance had blossomed. When the poems which he now wrote about Emma were published Florence saw the irony: as she wrote to a friend 'the idea of the general reader will be that TH's second marriage is a most disastrous one and that his sole wish is to find refuge in the grave with her with whom he alone found happiness'.

Hardy could still be charmed by an attractive woman and such a one was Gertrude Bugler, an amateur actress who appeared in several dramatizations of his books presented in Dorchester. He involved himself quite closely with these amateur players, though he was unhappy with most of the professional productions based on his books. For them he wrote *The Famous Tragedy of the Queen of Cornwall*, which for Hardy embodied something of Emma. His first visit to Cornwall made him think of writing something based on the story of Tristram and Iseult and he revived the idea after a trip there with Florence in 1916, though the play was not finished until 1923.

Hardy was unhappy with others' attempts at writing his biography and was guarded with those who sought to interview him about his life. Towards the end of the First World War he began to go through his papers and noted 'Put in Will that I have written no autobiography but that my wife has notes sufficient for a memoir'. In fact an almost complete autobiography was written, drawing on his records and his memories but presenting only what he wished to be known. As he finished working on papers they were destroyed, as was a manuscript as soon as Florence had typed it. Amendments to the typescript were made in disguised writing. Exactly how much contribution Florence made cannot be known, but the intention was to ascribe the work to her and later, only three weeks after Hardy's death, she was able to dispatch a 100,000 word typescript, *The Early Life of Thomas Hardy* to his publishers. Two years afterwards, *The Later Years* was delivered to complete the story of his life. Both were published under the name of Florence Hardy.

The First World War had seriously shaken Hardy's hopes and beliefs in the future of mankind, and he had aged considerably. His health was generally good, there was more concern for Florence who, in 1924, underwent an operation to remove a tumour. Like many elderly people he was becoming forgetful in day-to-day matters though his memories of the past were still vivid. Florence kept away most would-be visitors and carefully watched over him. One friend made in the post-war years who was always welcome, however, was T.E. Lawrence, 'Lawrence of Arabia', who wrote after seeing him in the spring of 1923:

'... *he is waiting so tranquilly for death, without a desire or ambition left in his spirit, as far as I can feel it: and yet he entertains so many illusions, and hopes for the world, things which I, in my disillusioned middle-age, feel to be illusory. They used to call this man a pessimist. While really he is full of fancy expectations.*'

In November 1927, when Hardy was revising poems for the collection *Winter Words*, among them a few new poems and some early very personal poems that had not previously been made public, he told Florence he had accomplished all he had set out to do: he went on working until 11 December. Going to his desk that day he found himself, for the first time, unable to work. Tired and weak he found he was able to get up for only a few hours each day and by the New Year he was deteriorating rapidly. He died on the morning of 11 January 1928 at 9.05 am.

Hardy almost certainly expected burial beside his family in Stinsford churchyard but Cockerell did not read this as strictly stipulated and negotiated with the Abbey. It was eventually arranged that his heart should be buried at Stinsford, the rest of his body being interred in Westminster Abbey.

The ceremonies took place on 16 January, with a third simultaneous memorial service at St. Peter's Church in Dorchester.

Thomas Hardy's study, recreated in Dorset County Museum as it was at his death. As well as his books and papers and the pens he used, the objects to be seen include the gown for a Doctor of Literature, bestowed by Cambridge University, his violin and his favourite walking stick.

HARDY'S WESSEX

Pilsdon Pen, looking south towards the sea.

Thomas Hardy appropriated Wessex as the name for the landscape of his imagination, but he did not invent it. Wessex was one of the ancient kingdoms of Britain. It was the kingdom of the West Saxons, invaders who came to Britain after the departure of the Romans. According to the Anglo-Saxon Chronicle, Vortigern, ruler of the former Roman province invited Jutish warriors led by Hengist and Horsa to come as mercenaries to help him against the northern Picts – but that being done, they stayed and forced the British out of Kent. It describes how other Saxons and Angles followed, conquering the British to set up three other kingdoms in what we know as England. In 495, Cerdic and his son Cynric landed in three little ships at the head of Southampton Water, in the centre of England's

southern coast, and conquered the territory around. That was the beginning of Wessex. Archaeological evidence suggests that the West Saxon people actually moved into this part of the country from the north-east, spreading outwards from the Wash. Information on the period between the departure of the Roman legionaries and the late 7th century, when Saxon settlers were firmly established, is thin and the Chronicle, written centuries later, is of questionable authority. But perhaps these particular leaders did arrive just where it says.

From the establishment of Cynric's son Ceawlin as king in 560, the record seems more reliable. He extended his power north of the River Thames, but over the centuries Wessex's borders

fluctuated. The kingdom spread westward, a Saxon monastery was established in Exeter before 690, but territory was lost to the Mercians in the north and at one time they even took possession of southern Hampshire. Wessex stretched from Cornwall to Kent but Danish invasion saw it shrink back again.

In all seven kingdoms developed in England, power passed between them with the strongest king becoming overlord. He was called Bretwalda, 'Ruler of Britain'. Early in the nineth century this was the Saxon, Egbert (802-839), but by the time of his death, all were under pressure from new invaders.

The first Viking raiders to lay claim to the Dorset coast landed in Weymouth Bay in 780. They were mistaken for a trading party but killed the royal official who attempted to escort them to King Brihtric in Dorchester. In the 790s there were raids on monasteries in Northumberland in the north of England, but it was not until the 830s that the Danish attackers came with any frequency. In 852, in Kent, they seized land and occupied it and in 866 a Danish army arrived in East Anglia intent on conquest.

The Danes forced their way through the other kingdoms and though, for a time, the West Saxons held them by battle or by treaty, a winter assault after a treaty, when the Wessex army returned home to bring in the harvest, saw them in control as far as Devon. Meanwhile, Wessex's King Alfred was lying low on the Isle of Altheney in the Somerset marshes. Victories by the Devon men, guerrilla attacks from Altheney and a secret mustering of the Wessex army led to a battle on the edge of Salisbury Plain where Alfred was the victor. The Danes left Wessex, but their leader became a Christian and stayed on to rule in East Anglia.

This was not the end of battles against the Danes, but Alfred recovered London and the re-conquest of Danish-held territory was completed by his grandson, Athelstan. From then on the kings of Wessex became the kings of England. Wessex no longer existed as an independent territory, and the name was rarely used until Hardy adopted it and made it once more familiar as the setting for his work.

Hardy's Wessex should not be confused with the ancient kingdom or with the specific counties of the south-west for it does not match any historic borders; when Hardy drew a map of *his* Wessex he carried it as far as Oxford, Windsor and Portsmouth to the east, and from Bristol to Launceston and Plymouth to the west. He divided this territory, following the old county borders of the time (there have been boundary changes and new counties created since), into several regions which he called South, North, Upper, Mid, Outer and Lower Wessex (corresponding to Dorset, Berkshire, Hampshire, Wiltshire, Somerset and Devon) with Cornwall designated Off Wessex or Lyonnesse.

Hardy's Wessex embraces more than half of southern England. It varies enormously in terrain, from wild Dartmoor and gentle water meadows to craggy sea-pounded cliffs and wind-swept Salisbury Plain. There are no high mountains and no great cities (though Hardy lived in London and wrote about it, it does not form part of his personal landscape): his Wessex offers areas of extreme isolation and sleepy villages as well as lively resorts along the coast.

The Valency Valley of Cornwall, the setting of *A Pair of Blue Eyes* and of great importance in his own life, Oxford 'Christminster', with the Berkshire towns of Reading 'Aldbrickham', Wantage 'Alfredston', and Newbury 'Kennetbridge', where so much of his last novel *Jude the Obscure* took place, are the extremities of the fictional Wessex. The county of Devon makes little contribution to the major novels, though it is the location of some stories and poems. Somerset (the old county that is, much of which is now assigned to Avon) includes the beautiful Georgian city of Bath, Wells 'Fountall', with its fine cathedral, Taunton 'Toneborough' and mysterious Glastonbury 'Glaston'. Wiltshire is home to the ancient circle of Stonehenge where Tess was arrested, elegant Wilton House, seat of the Earls of Pembroke, the setting for 'The Marchioness of Stonehenge' (one of the *Noble Dames*), and of course Salisbury 'Melchester', with its cathedral spire pointing up to God, is a building which Hardy held in great affection. Salisbury features in several poems and stories, in *Two on a Tower* and *The Hand of Ethelberta*. In *Jude*, Sue Bridehead, like Hardy's sisters, goes to training college. In Hampshire, the coastal towns and New Forest provide some locations. 'Lady Mottisfont' (another *Noble Dame*) is set in Broadlands 'Deansleigh Park' and Winchester 'Witoncester' is where Tess is hanged; Jude goes to Basingstoke 'Stoke Barehills', and it is at Weyhill 'Weydon Priors' that the fair takes place where Michael Henchard sells his wife, initiating the tragic history of *The Mayor of Casterbridge*.

The heart of Hardy's Wessex, where so much of his story-telling is set, is his home county of Dorset, especially those areas where he lived and knew particularly well. They have their own section later in this book.

In one poem, 'Wessex Heights', not a poem about landscape, but about his feelings for the lost loves of his life, he nevertheless encompasses his whole

world: the 'grey Plain' and the 'tall spire' of Salisbury, the 'Froom-side Vale', 'Yell'ham Bottom' and other lowlands where memories haunt him and the high places 'Where men have never cared to haunt, nor women have walked with me': Inkpen Beacon, Wills-Neck, 'homely Bulbarrow' and 'little Pilsdon Crest'. Wills-Neck is the highest point of the Quantocks in the west, Inkpen is in Berkshire, Bul-

mysterious way it is the land itself that has helped to mould him and his characters, and it is a part of all of them. So to is the history of Wessex. He remembers

' ... *where Vespasian's legions struck the sands,*
And Cerdic with his Saxons entered in,
And Henry's army leapt afloat to win
Convincing triumphs over neighbour lands ...'

Bulbarrow, looking south-west as evening draws in. As on so many Wessex heights the hilltop is ridged by the mounds and ditches of an earthwork fortification.

barrow is in the centre of Dorset and Pilsdon Pen in its south-west.

Hardy's poem is about people and emotions and though in verse he may vividly conjure up the swallow diving over the river at Sturminster or in his prose describe a view as it appears to his characters, he almost never indulges in description for its own sake. In some

He was well-acquainted with local custom and folk magic, with tales of smuggling, bloodshed and of country festivals and the hard life of the farm worker: that multi-faceted background of human experience is the major part of Hardy's Wessex.

That history goes back long before the Romans came. This was one of the earliest parts of England to be settled and it is rich in prehistoric monuments. Flint tools found in Dorset may date back 80,000 years and a stone shelter on Portland has been dated at 5,200 B.C. The caves at Cheddar in Somerset's Mendip Hills sheltered prehistoric people 12,000 years ago, and at nearby Wookey, layer upon layer has been excavated, indicating alternate human and animal occupation, for the

works survive. Long barrows were used for group burials, some have stone chambers within the piled earth oval. Circular earthworks with a ditch inside, probably with a ritual purpose were also made, and on the edge of Cranborne Chase, not far from Sixpenny Hadley, are two parallel ditches and banks that run for more than 10 km (6½ miles), whose significance is unknown. There is a shorter cursus in Wiltshire, near Stonehenge,

Eggardon Hill, east of Bridport, the 'Haggerdon Hill' of *The Trumpet Major.*

bones of long extinct mammoths and sabre-toothed tigers have been found: in the same locations are situated awe-inspiring caves with spectacular stalactites and stalagmites.

From about 4,000 B.C. onwards, the Neolithic inhabitants were beginning to develop agriculture and from that period many long barrows and other earth-

and at about this date the first of the circles of that famous monument were erected.

In the Bronze Age the barrows became circular in form, in which grave goods of gold, amber and Dorset Kimmeridge shale have been found alongside the skeletons and cremated remains.

RIGHT

Maiden Castle, the massive hill fort about 3 km (2 miles) from Dorchester. There was a causewayed enclosure here in Neolithic times and after being deserted and used for barrow burials, was re-fortified in the Iron Age, first as a single rampart ringing the hill as far as the path seen crossing the hill. Later this was extended to enclose the full area; two outer ramparts were built and the complicated entrance-ways constructed.

BELOW

The scale of the ramparts and ditches made them extremely difficult to storm.

LEFT

The Cerne Abbas Giant, cut into the hillside turf is 54 m (180 ft) from top to toe, his knobbly club 36 m (120 ft). He seems to be an obvious fertility symbol, but when was he made? There is evidence that he once had a cloak over his left arm and this may suggest a British variation of Hercules, which would correspond with the late Roman or early post-Roman period 1,500-1,600 years ago. There is no mention of the figure in medieval documents regarding Cerne, indeed no mention at all until the 18th century, thus raising doubts as to its ancient origin. Local people must have placed value on his presence, for such figures require regular cleaning out to keep the image sharp. In an area where mystical and magical belief has been strong this is not perhaps surprising, and it is said that as late as the 19th century local women believed that sleeping on the hill would cure infertility. A rectangular earthwork higher up the hill may have no connection with the giant, but until 1635 it was a place where a maypole was erected – another fertility symbol.

LEFT

The 14th-century tithe barn at Cerne Abbas, partly converted into a house in the 18th century, was said by Hardy to be the model for the one which he described in *Far from the Madding Crowd.*

In the Iron Age there was more pressure on land and competition for territory between tribal groups and many hilltops were turned into defensive forts which may also have become centres for administering the area. There are more than 30 in Dorset alone, of which the best known are Maiden Castle and Cadbury. On the uplands, field patterns still survive from this time, well over 2,000 years ago, and there were many farmsteads and small settlements: some people, however, were beginning to occupy the hill forts more permanently like towns, what the invading Romans called *oppida*. In Dorset the people called themselves the Durotriges, they had a port at Hengistbury Head from which they traded with continental Europe and the Roman world.

The Romans invaded in A.D. 43 and Vespasian's Second Legion overcame the natives in their hill forts – in the war cemetery within Maiden Castle a skeleton was found with a Roman spearhead still lodged in the vertebrae – which were deserted as the Romans began to establish towns.

Legend tells how Joseph of Arimathea, in whose tomb the body of Jesus Christ was laid, came to preach the gospel in Britain and brought the Holy Grail to Glastonbury, burying it beneath what is known as the Chalice Spring. His staff, pressed into the ground as he leaned upon it, took root and flowered. The original tree, on

Stonehenge, one of the world's most famous monuments, where Tess of the d'Urbervilles was arrested for killing her husband.

The outer bank and ditch, the oldest part of this circular structure, encloses a circle of stones and the 'heelstone' beyond it to the north-east which date from before 2150 B.C. But the structure has gone through several transformations since. About 1675 B.C., a double circle of 80 bluestones, brought more than 320 km (200 miles) from South Wales, was set up and an approach avenue created leading north-eastwards. About a quarter of a century later they were taken down and two circles of stones, brought from the Marlborough Downs, were erected with lintel stones across the top of them.

Weary-All Hill, was cut down during the Civil War, but cuttings from it are still said to flower among the abbey ruins in Glastonbury. Glastonbury, once an island, is often said to be the legendary Avalon, to which King Arthur's body was taken, and the monks of the abbey once claimed a grave here to be that of Arthur. All that can be certain is that a prominent person was buried there in the period after the Romans left when Arthur, or his historical counterpart, was fighting o keep back the Saxons.

Abbey and town stand at the foot of Glastonbury Tor, a cone-shaped hill which many consider lies at the conjunction of ley lines thus concentrating their power. From its top, looking south-east across the Somerset Levels where prehistoric lake villages have been found, Cadbury Hill fort can be seen. This was re-fortified in the fifth and sixth centuries giving some plausibility to the claim that this was Arthur's Camelot. Another legend has it that Arthur and his knights lie sleeping here until the day arrives when their country needs them and that every seven years the hillside opens and they ride out to water their horses at a spring near Sutton Montis church. Across, on the other side of Wessex, in Winchester, Arthur's supposed Round Table can be seen displayed in the Great Hall of the castle – though it dates from about 1150, not from Arthur's time.

A great many of today's Wessex villages appear to have been established in Saxon times and are listed in the Domesday Book, the record of the kingdom made for William I in 1080 after the Normans had conquered Saxon England. The Normans built castles, such as those at Sherbourne and Corfe, and the middle ages saw the growth of rich monastic foundations. But for the peasant, life was probably little changed, even by the transfer of

At the summer solstice, the sun rises directly over the heelstone casting its shadow towards the centre. A structure which involved such planning, time and effort in its making was obviously of great importance: but what was it for? It may have been built for a purely ritual purpose, but it has been suggested that it was used for making astronomical calculations and that it was a form of computer. Later still, some of the bluestones were arranged in a line between the capped circles and in an inner horseshoe.

The tower is all that now remains of the 15th-century Church of St. Michael on the top of conical Glastonbury Tor. Visible for long distances across the surrounding countryside, it is not surprising that this site has been thought to be endowed with special powers. This was once an island and despite the many drainage dykes or 'rhines' many places in marshy Sedgemoor can still be cut off by flooding or by winter snows.

monastic lands to secular owners, until the enclosure of the land by property owners and the mechanization of agriculture, though the industrial revolution ruined small cottage industries.

The rural population would have been little interested in the outcome of 12th-century battles, the royal strife between Stephen and Matilda or the dynastic struggles of the Wars of the Roses, but Wessex was divided by the struggle between King and Parliament and in the Civil War, towns and castles were besieged. Both armies tended to exploit the land and a party developed with the motto 'If you take our cattle / We will give you battle': they were thoroughly disenchanted with war and supported neither faction. They called themselves the Clubmen and a group of

ABOVE
Portesham House, in the village below Blackdown, the home of Admiral Hardy until 1807. He was the Captain of Nelson's flagship *HMS Victory*, the man who held the dying Nelson in his arms when he spoke his last words 'Kiss me Hardy'. His novelist namesake liked to think of himself as a member of the same family.

LEFT
A strange chimney-shaped structure is the tower erected as a monument to Admiral Sir Thomas Masterman Hardy (1769-1839) on Blackdown, between Dorchester and Abbotsbury. It has a fine viewpoint, and is visible from Hardy's Max Gate home.

OPPOSITE
Looking east from Ryall in south-
west Dorset.

2,000 established themselves in the earthworks on Hambledon Hill, near Shaftesbury, where they were routed by the Cromwellians in 1645.

Half a century later, there was considerable local support when the Duke of Monmouth landed to claim the throne. After his defeat at Sedgemoor and the 'bloody assize', conducted by Judge Jeffreys at Dorchester and Winchester, there were mass executions. At Dorchester alone 74 rebels were hung and quartered, their heads impaled on the church railings and parts of their bodies distributed to towns around to be displayed as a warning to others.

The Jacobite campaigns of the 18th century in support of the Stuart succession had little affect here in the south of England: but with the threat of French invasion during the Napoleonic Wars the coastal lands of Wessex prepared themselves to meet Boney's attack with the creation of local militia (akin to the Home Guard of the Second World War). Hill-top beacons were got ready to send a signal of fire across the land. Hardy was born only 25 years after the Battle of Waterloo and as a boy those times would have been fresh in the memories of his older relations. As he himself recalled, there were still many visible reminders from doors riddled with bullet holes used for target practice, ridges on the down from entrenchments thrown up by soldiers to tattered uniforms and rotting pike shafts.

Hardy had a profound sense of the history and the life of the land from which he came. Consciously, he often drew upon this knowledge in his writing, but it forms a deeper, more fundamental background, both to his own life, and the creation of his work.

RIGHT
In the Frome Valley in Dorset,
Hardy's 'Valley of the Great
Dairies', the water meadows were
deliberately flooded to keep them
fertile and well-watered.
(See pages 66-68)

DORCHESTER

Grey's Bridge, built in 1748, carries the London Road over the Frome outside the town. This is the bridge of the poem 'Sitting on a Bridge', about girls sitting on the parapet flirting with soldiers from the Dorchester barracks.

Dorchester is the 'Casterbridge' of Hardy's famous novel. The fair at which the mayor sells his wife at the beginning of the story and where, some 18 years later, she goes to look for him, is many miles away at Weydon Priors (which can be identified with Weyhill, in northern Hampshire, half-way between Salisbury and Reading: but it is in Casterbridge that most of the story of Michael Henchard takes place.

Here, within half-an-hour's walk, or so, of his Brockhampton birthplace, Hardy went to school and worked in John Hicks's architects's office. He lived in Shire-Hall Place from 1883 until he moved into Max Gate, on the outskirts of the town, where he lived until his death. He became a local magistrate and, in 1910, a Freeman of the Borough, His statue stands at 'Top O' Town' (see page 7) and the Country Museum (designed by his employer

G.R. Crickmay) houses an important collection of his books and manuscripts and a reconstruction of the study in which he wrote.

Casterbridge is the Dorchester of the 1840s and 1850s, the town Hardy knew as a boy. It differs a little from the actual town, a building's location being sometimes altered or invented, but even today much of it is recognizable, if one is able to ignore the modern shop frontages on the older houses, the traffic and street furniture. Now, as then, it is a busy country town rather than a museum piece, and in its back streets especially, you can find many unspoilt 18th- and 19th-century houses. There is little left from earlier periods. Dorchester has often been ravaged by fire. In 1613, a conflagration which began in the house of a tallow chandler destroyed a large part of the timber-framed medieval town and was followed by others in 1622, 1725, 1732, 1775, 1779 and 1789 before better fire

fighting arrangements were established. Hardy's own time saw much rebuilding: the Corn Exchange was not built until 1848 and the florid clock tower was added in 1864. All Saints' Church, with its tall spire did not appear until 1843 and St. Peter's, dating partly from the 12th century and mainly from the 15th was extensively restored, Hardy himself drawing the plans for the architect in charge, John Hicks. A little furthur up the High Street, the County Museum, despite its frontage in perpendicular style, was not built until 1844. Even the medieval Napier's Almshouses in South Street (locally known as Napper's Mite) had their frontage rebuilt in similar style in 1842. Yet Dorchester has a history as old as any town or city in Britain.

It is not known if there was a settlement here before the Romans came but there were certainly people hereabouts. The great hill fort of Maiden Castle is only about 3 km (less than 2 miles) south-west from the town centre. A similar hill fort, Poundbury, is closer to the north-west and a neolithic henge monument, Maumbury Rings, is actually within the modern town. The Romans probably set up a hill fort or military camp by the River Frome before establishing the town of Durnovaria, but by 70 A.D. everyone had moved down from Maiden Castle and it had become an important urban centre. It was enclosed by a rhomboid of earthwork defences with west and east walls at right-angles and a shorter eastern wall joined on the north by an angled wall roughly following the line of the Frome. In the 4th century, these were surmounted by stone walls. Only one tiny section of the wall can be seen today but the location of the walls is roughly that of the avenue of shaded walks which surrounds the old town that was laid out on the top of the

This cast metal sign appears on many of Dorset's old bridges, a reminder of the harsh punishments of the first half of the 19th century and of the fate of the Tolpuddle Martyrs.

Maumbury Rings, a prehistoric ridge and ditch earthwork built for ritual purposes rather than as a fort. The Romans converted it into an amphitheatre, lowering the level inside by 3 m (10 ft), cutting into the chalk to form walls and installing wooden seating on tiers: they also formed antechambers where animals or contestants were held while waiting to go into the arena. During the Civil War it was further modified to turn it into a fort to defend the Weymouth road. In the 18th century it became the site of the town gallows, giving huge crowds a good view of hangings from its circular banks. In *The Mayor of Casterbridge,* Hardy makes this the place where Henchard arranges to meet Susan.

Roman bank in the 18th century. The foundations of the houses are visible in Colliton Park, within the north-west corner of the walls, and excavations have revealed public baths and other buildings: but not only have the upper parts of the structures disappeared, their very foundations seem to have been dug out, presumably so that the materials could be used for new building. There was a public water supply brought by aqueduct several miles up the River Frome, the channel having been cut into the earth and following the contours of the land rather then carried on arches: Maumbury Rings was turned into an amphitheatre for public entertainment. On route from London to Exeter it became a local market centre with a wider trade in pottery, shale and marble obtained from the quarries further along the coast.

Nowhere do the present streets follow the Roman layout precisely and the town may have become deserted after the Romans left; but as Saxon Dorwaraceaster, it became the centre of a royal estate with a palace and mint which was established by Athelstan, son of Alfred the Great. The Domesday Book records that it had 172 houses.

The Normans built a castle, though nothing of it survives, and in the middle ages it became a weaving and trading centre for broadcloth, and developed a still-flourishing brewery industry – Dorchester ale has been famous for centuries.

In the 17th century John White, the rector of Holy Trinity and St. Peter's, was the promoter and organizer of a settlement in Massachusetts, first known as New Dorchester, raising the necessary money and a charter from King Charles I. Puritan feeling in the town was strong and it began by supporting Parliament against the King in the Civil War, though surrendering when it came under Royalist attack – only to be recaptured by the Cromwellians.

In 1685, after the defeat of the Monmouth Rebellion, Judge Jeffreys set up court in a room behind the Antelope in South Street. Over 300 people were tried there, the evidence against some so-called rebels being no more than that they had been away from their homes at

the time of the rebellion. Some were transported to plantations in the Caribbean, some sent to local prisons (where conditions were such that 18 died of fever within three months) and 74 were executed with great barbarity as a warning to all the populace.

Only a few years before Hardy himself was born, Dorchester again earned a place in history, and especially the history of the Trade Union movement when the Court Room in the Shire Hall was the setting for the trial of six local men who became known as the 'Tolpuddle Martyrs'. They were a group

early forms of trade unions were known. A depression in trade in 1829, and the continuing introduction of ever more steam-driven machinery, replacing what had been rural cottage workers in trades such as weaving, and the use of women and children at cheaper rates to operate it, led to a new outbreak of unrest which was savagely put down. By 1831, an agricultural worker earned only enough to buy ten loaves of bread a week, without allowing for such luxuries as other food, clothes or fuel.

Betrayed by an informer, who attended a society initiation ceremony

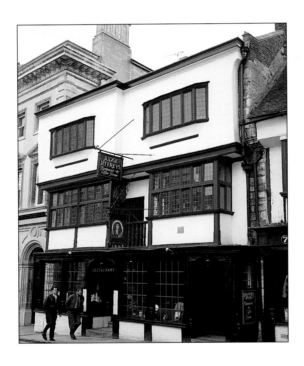

of farm workers, led by George Loveless and his brother James, who in 1833-4 (six years before Hardy was born) formed a Friendly Society in an attempt to counter reductions of their wages to only eight, then seven and soon just only six shillings per week.

The American and French Revolutions and a naval mutiny at the end of the 18th century had put the landowners and governing classes of Britain in fear of a popular rising and led to repressive new laws against 'combinations', as the

posing as an applicant for admission, the six founder members were arrested.

Peaceable men, their rules specifically stated 'that the objects of this society can never be promoted by any acts of violence'; all but one being Methodists and several lay preachers, they walked quietly with the local constable to Dorchester and jail. They were tried under an act of 1825 for conspiracy against the Common Law and the judge also invoked a statute passed to deal with the naval mutinies of 1796-7: they were sentenced to seven years transportation 'for administering an illegal oath'.

Their case became a national *cause célèbre* for what had been done to them could be done to many more. The 1832 Parliamentary Reform Bill, which began the first extension of the right to vote had been passed after much agitation and a huge demonstration in London. A great procession was organized in support of the Tolpuddle Martyrs: 20,000-30,000 people marched through London in complete silence to take part in a meeting of 20,000, giving the police and military who had been mobilized no excuse to

sixth, James Hammet, returned to Tolpuddle. When old and blind he became a burden to his family and went to the poorhouse to die, as so many agricultural workers did. He is buried in the churchyard at Tolpuddle.

Hardy himself must have known Dorchester from a very early age and from Michaelmas 1850 he attended the British School established by the British and Foreign Bible Society and run by Isaac Last in Greyhound Yard.

On the four-kilometre walk to school each day, the schoolboy had to pass by the slums of Fordington on the outskirts

LEFT
The Old Crown Court in the Shire Hall, where the Tolpuddle Martyrs were tried on 17 March 1834. The Judge sat under the canopy with the Royal Arms and the accused were placed in the box in the centre of the courtroom.

arrest or attack them. A petition signed by 250,000 called for their release but it took another two years of constant pressure before anything was done – and then the Tolpuddle convicts who had been shipped out to the penal colony of Tasmania were not told and it was a further two years before they were returned to England.

A collection of £1,300 was raised to establish five of them in Essex on their return (though they were said to have eventually emigrated to Canada). The

of Dorchester, home of paupers and prostitutes, where the Evangelical Rev. Henry Moule was vicar at St. George's.

The Rev. Moule and his family won considerable public gratitude for their role in fighting and controlling a cholera epidemic which developed in Fordington in 1854 during Hardy's childhood. (His life and that of the owners of the local brewery were dramatized in David Edgar's play *Entertaining Strangers* which was originally written as a community play for the town of Dorchester.)

ABOVE
The Kings Arms Hotel in High East Street. In *The Mayor of Casterbridge,* Michael Henchard is entertaining his friends in the first floor room when he is seen through the open bow window by his wife Elizabeth-Jane: in a front room on the ground floor the bankruptcy commissioners meet to deal with his financial failure.

RIGHT
Standfast or Prince's Bridge, crossing the Frome at Fordington, with St. George's on the hill above. This is the fictional Durnover. This is the end of Cuckold Row and an ancient mill once stood by the river here; but the original slum district is no longer recognizable, replaced by neat artisans' houses in the last half of the 19th century and with many attractive older buildings preserved, it is now a pleasant place to live.

The epidemic was a major cause for improving and replacing the squalid living conditions of the area which helped the epidemic to spread.

Hardy became a friend of the rector's sons and was much influenced by them as a young man. He possibly got to know them through his employer or through William Barnes, the poet, who ran a school in the house next door to Hicks's office in South Street at the time that Hardy was articled there. Barnes, who was highly regarded by Hardy, also became a friend and as rector of Came was within easy walking distance of Hardy's home at Max Gate.

Before moving to the Max Gate house, Hardy and Emma lived in Dorchester at Shire-Hall Place, in a house which had previously been the residence of the headmaster of Dorset County School. It stood in what is now Glyde Path Road, where there is a health clinic today. It was entered through an arch and a passageway so there is no street frontage for it stretched behind the buildings on the High Street.

That house has gone, but Max Gate is owned by the National Trust and is open to visitors for part of the year.

LEFT
The house identified with that in which Michael Henchard lived.

BELOW
The former Rectory at Came, just outside Dorchester and within a short walk across the fields from Hardy's home at Max Gate, was the last home of his friend William Barnes, the dialect poet whom he so much admired.

THE BLACKMORE VALE

Shaftesbury 'Shaston', looking from Park Walk over the lower town around St. James's church and out over the Vale to Marnhull 'Marlott' and Sturminster Newton 'Stourcastle'.

The Blackmore Vale, the 'Vale of the Little Dairies' of *Tess of the d'Urbervilles,* lies to the north of the chalk hills that run through Dorset from the south-east up to Cranborne Chase. It is watered by the River Stour and its tributaries, the river cutting through chalk escarpment at the gap by Hambledon Hill, defended by its hill fort and that on neighbouring Hod Hill, to flow on through Blandford Forum and Wimborne Minster to reach the sea at Hengistbury Head and Christchurch.

Hardy describes the valley as 'a broad rich mass of grass and trees, mantling minor hills and dales' and contrasts its small fields with their pattern of dark hedges with the huge fields and open spaces of the surrounding hills. The ground drops steeply over 120m (400 ft) to the north of the chalk escarpment and the clay soil of the valley provides lush pasture for its dairy herds. The valley settlements keep clear of the river banks and are set a little higher to avoid the risk of frequent flooding. As Hardy wrote in *Tess*, the secret of

Blackmoor (either spelling is correct and it has also been called the Vale of the White Hart) is 'best discovered from the heights around', not just Hambledon but Bulbarrow, Nettlecombe Tout, Dogbury, High Stoy and Bubb Down, while to the north the vale is overlooked by Shaftesbury.

Hardy once thought of taking a house in Shaftesbury but decided instead on Swanage: he thought it had such bracing air that one day it would become a popular resort. At Shaftesbury, as 'Shaston' he sets the opening of the fourth part of *Jude the Obscure* and it is at Ox House, 'Old Grove's Place' in Bimport, that he sets Sue's home after her marriage to Mr. Phillotson.

Shaftesbury is unusual in this region for it is a hill town. Its steep and picturesque Gold Hill has been much photographed and has become familiar to people who have no idea where it is, as a film and television location. Alfred the Great founded a nunnery here for one of his daughters in the 9th century and probably the fortified settlement from which the town developed as well. The bones of Edward the Martyr, a Saxon boy king, were buried here, and it became a shrine for pilgrimage, forgotten after the dissolution of the monasteries and rediscovered in 1931.

Some 8 km (five miles) south-west of Shaftesbury, set above the Stour is the large and rather rambling village of Marnhull, the 'Marlott' which was Tess's home village. Its Crown Inn is the 'Pure Drop Inn' of the story, but the house traditionally known as Tess's Cottage may not be the one which Hardy envisaged as the home of the Durbeyfields. The bridge over the Stour still bears a notice from the 1820s warning that anyone found guilty of damaging it will be liable to transportation for life. It is a reminder of the

sentence given to the Tolpuddle Martyrs and is a sign that appears on many bridges erected by the county.

Further down the Stour, built on a spur of higher ground above a meander in the river, is the market town of Sturminster Newton, Hardy's 'Stourcastle'. It is the focus of the Vale and though usually a quiet and sleepy place becomes busy and noisy on Mondays when one of England's major cattle markets is held here.

Hardy lived here at Riverside Villas during one of the happiest periods of his

Gold Hill, Shaftesbury. There are cottages on only one side of this steep, curving, cobbled street, the other is a buttressed medieval wall.

BELOW
Tess Cottage at Marnhull,
identified by many as the original
for the Durbeyfield home.

life. His house overlooks an island in the Stour and he rowed on the river here. Not far away is Newton Mill, part 17th- and part 18th-century, which is still in operation, a weir ensuring a strong pressure of water for its wheel. When the Stour was in flood from incessant rain, Hardy noted how lumps of froth floated down 'like swans' and accumulated against the bridge.

Sturminster was where William Barnes, the local dialect poet so much admired by Hardy, was baptized, went to school and was first employed as a solicitor's clerk. Hardy, who grew up surrounded by the local speech and was

BELOW
The Church and Crown Hotel at
Marnhull, which becomes 'Marlott'
with its 'Pure Drop Inn' in *Tess of
the d'Urbervilles.*

constantly pressured by his mother not
to speak or act like the country people
and to make an effort to 'better himself',
may well have been careful to avoid elements of dialect creeping into his speech
when making his way in the world. But
he tried to reflect it in some of his dia-
logue as an important aspect of Wessex
life. These few lines by Barnes, if pro-
nounced just as they are written, will
give some idea of the sound. Hardy
would surely have agreed with its sentiments:

*'Vor to breed the young fox or the heäre
We can gi'e up whole eäcres o' ground;
But the greens be a-gadged, vor to rear*

Looking over Melbury Bubb from Bubb Down.

Our young children up healthy an' sound,
Why, there woont be a-left the next age
A green spot where their veet can goo free:
An' the goocoo wull soon be committed
    to cage
Vor a trespass in zomebody's tree.'

Or try this:
'In the zunsheen of our zummers
Wi' the hay time now a-come'
How busy wer we out a-vield
Wi' vew a-left at hwome ...'

The Vale proper is mainly to the north of Sturminster Newton, but Hardy includes the farms and orchards much further east and south-east across to the slopes of High Stoy and Bubb Down, and it is here that much of *The Woodlanders* is set. In its first printing it takes place around Bubb Down, but in revising it for later editions he moved the location eastwards to the region of High Stoy, though altering details to make the setting fit the story. Melbury Osmond is where Hardy's mother, Jemima, was born and in the church here, overlooking the Vale, she was married to his father. It is a contender for the original 'Little Hintock', though Hardy himself denied any direct link and would only say that it included features from several villages, including Melbury Bubb, 'all lying more or less under the eminence called High-Stoy'.

Sherborne, Thomas Hardy's Sherton Abbas'), provides a market for Giles Winterborne, the Castle which Grace Melbury visits and the 'Abbey north of Blackmore Vale' where they talk of their future. It is beyond the Vale on the River Yeo, but the town for this locality (though Yeovil in Somerset is not much further).

This was the seat of the Saxon Bishops of Wessex and the town still has the air of a cathedral city. The magnificent Abbey church, with its fine fan vaulting, has Saxon, Norman and Perpendicular features and other parts of the abbey survive in the buildings of Sherborne School. There are ancient almshouses, 16th-century and earlier timber-framed dwellings and Georgian houses and not just one, but two castles. The first, the 12th-century fortified palace of the Bishop of Salisbury was bought by Sir Walter Raleigh, who began the building of the second, which was added to by various owners after Raleigh's execution. The old castle was besieged by Parliamentary forces in the Civil War and it was their mining, rather than decay, that brought about its present ruin.

BELOW
Melbury Osmond Church. Hardy's parents were married here, in the village where Jemima lived as a child. The final scene of *The Woodlanders* has Marty South alone in the churchyard, though in revising the book Hardy shifted its location eastwards.

BOTTOM
Sherborne Castle, built in the early 12th century. This is the setting for Hardy's Civil War tale 'Anna Lady Baxby' and along with the rest of Sherborne as 'Sherton Abbas' features in *The Woodlanders*.

61

EGDON HEATH & THE VALLEYS OF THE FROME & PIDDLE

OPPOSITE

Evershot, at the head of the river Frome, is the 'Evershead' where Tess rested on her way to Beaminster 'Emminster' and breakfasted at this cottage by the church.

BELOW

Rainbarrow Hill. 'Egdon Heath' still surrounds the pastureland of the valley.

Once there may have been a great sweep of heathland that stretched across much of Dorset, but the advance of agriculture, forestation and, latterly, of urbanization, had broken it into many separated heaths, each with its own name, long before Hardy chose to link them all together under the name of Egdon Heath. His Egdon runs from close by his Bockhampton birthplace to Poole Harbour and beyond, and through it flows the River Frome (or Froom, as Hardy spells it) creating his Vale of the Great Dairies.

The Frome rises above Evershot and then passes through Maiden Newton. Before reaching Dorchester and flowing below the town it is joined by the Cerne, which rises on the other side of Batcombe and comes down through Cerne Abbas. At Dorchester the stream divides into more than one channel and continues to do so through much of the Vale. Past Stinsford and Bockhampton, at West Stafford, the Winterborne flows in from the south and after Woodsford the river divides and meets again before reaching Wool, Bindon Abbey, Wareham, and finally the sea at Poole Harbour.

Westward of Cerne Abbas and following a course roughly parallel north of the Frome is the River Piddle, the villages on it reflecting the variants on its name: Piddletrenthide, Piddlehinton, Puddletown, Tolpuddle and Briantspuddle. Between the two streams rise

ABOVE
Waterston Manor, near
Puddletown, the original for
Bathsheba Everdene's
'Weatherbury Farm'.

the higher land of Rainbarrow and Gallows Hill and to the south the downs separate the valley from the coast.

This is an area in which Hardy set large parts of his novels and stories and which inspired many poems. *Under the Greenwood Tree*, his story of the Mellstock Quire, the soon to be redundant church musicians and singers, and the love of one of them for the new school teacher, begins in the lane between Upper and Lower Bockhampton 'Upper and Lower Mellstock' and, except for one cart ride to Weymouth, all takes place in the vicinity of Hardy's birthplace which becomes Tranter Dewy's cottage and Keeper Day's house is in Yellowham Wood. Rising behind the Hardy cottage

is Rainbarrow Hill, with its tumulus, where a beacon was prepared ready to signal if the French invasion came in *The Dynasts* and where the 5 November bonfire is lit in *The Return of the Native* (though in that book he somewhat changes its location to a more central position on the heath.)

Desperate Remedies, which draws on his own experience as a church architect in Weymouth, takes only some elements from Bockhampton as 'Carriford', a location which occurs only in this novel, though the local Kingston Maurward House becomes 'Knapwater House' and Tolpuddle 'Tolchurch', where Owen Grey works on the church restoration.

Far from the Madding Crowd again

Puddletown Church. As 'Weatherbury', Puddletown has associations with leading events in *Far from the Madding Crowd,* but of particular interest are the box pews and gallery which dates from 1695. In such a gallery, the 'Mellstock quire' performed at Sunday services, though the one in which Hardy's father and grandfather played in at Stinsford was removed, according to *The Early Life of Thomas Hardy,* perhaps when the choir was disbanded about 1841: but others have claimed that it remained in position until about 1880.

uses Yellowham 'Yalbury' Wood and its cottage. Following the road over Yellowham Hill down to the River Piddle brings the traveller to Puddletown 'Weatherbury'. Time has changed it somewhat and, as so often, Hardy made changes in his fictional version, but here is the church where Troy spent the night and where Fanny Robin was buried. The church still retains its old box pews and the gallery where the musicians used to play at services just as the Mellstock Quire did. Such a gallery, which Hardy would have remembered from personal experience, was removed from Stinsford church when the choir was disbanded in about 1841.

In *Far from the Madding Crowd,* Hardy places Bathsheba Everdene's Jacobean house west of the church and close enough for children to be seen playing in the churchyard, but the actual house he had in mind is Waterston Manor, upstream of the village at some six times that distance from it.

A little further down the Piddle is Tolpuddle, famous for the farm workers who tried to organize against the harsh terms dictated by their employers.

Leaving the river and keeping on the main road to Poole, passing the hill variously known as Rings Hill or Weatherby Castle with its Iron Age earthworks where Hardy places the Welland Tower of *Two on a Tower* (there is no real tower, only an obelisk, tapering among the trees) brings one to Bere Regis. Beyond the village rises Woodbury Hill, the 'Greenhill' of *Far from the Madding Crowd*, where the annual sheep fair took place making this 'the Nijni Novgorod of South Wessex' as Hardy puts it, though the real fair was still held until well into the 20th century. The fair is said to have begun when a travelling packman, his goods having been soaked by a storm, spread his cloths and woollens out on the hill to dry. They stimulated the curiosity of the villagers who, seeing them flapping on the hill, who went up to investigate and bought all the packman's stock. Finding this a perfect ploy for attracting trade from the villagers, the man came back, and so did others until the fair developed into a three-week event before the competition of newer markets eclipsed its popularity. From Woodbury, the view west is over the hilly country where so much of *Far from the Madding Crowd* is set, back towards Dorchester and beyond.

In the parish church of Bere Regis 'Kingsbere' itself can be seen the family tombs of the Turberville family, the same which, allowing for Hardy's modification of the name, made Tess think of her d'Urberville lineage. It was outside the stained glass window with the Turberville coats-of-arms that Tess and her family set up their four-poster bed when they found that the rooms they had planned to stay in had already been let: but it is along the Frome that more of her story takes place.

In contrast to her native Blackmore Vale, Tess found the Frome valley much larger in scale. 'The enclosures numbered fifty acres instead of ten, the farmsteads were more extended, the groups of cattle formed tribes hereabouts; there only families.' Here were huge herds with their great udders hanging full come milking-time, raised on the fertile meadows.

This valley, surrounded by wild heath is conjured up by Hardy when he describes Angel Clare's return from his parent's home in 'Emminster' (Beaminster), looking out, probably from Frome Hill (only a mile from Hardy's house at Max Gate), over this 'green trough of sappiness and humidity':

'Immediately he began to descend from the upland to the fat alluvial soil below, the atmosphere grew heavier; the languid perfume of the summer fruits, the mists, the hay, the flowers, formed therein a vast pool of odour which at this hour seemed to make the animals, the very bees and butterflies drowsy.'

Writing about his Valley of the Great Dairies draws from Hardy an evocation of its atmosphere and seasons as detailed as any in his work, down to the marks left by cows where they lay down on the grass at night. Heady prose brimful with his own involvement as he celebrates his native landscape.

BELOW
Woodbury Hill, near Bere Regis, the 'Greenhill' of *Far from the Madding Crowd*, where the real sheep fair was held, and where Troy appears as Dick Turpin in the circus.

The lushness of the vale was maintained by skilful management and owed much to the skill of the 'drowner'. In wet months, when the river is flowing full, it floods out across the low-lying meadowland, making the pasture look more like paddy fields; but in Hardy's time, as he describes, this flooding was carefully controlled by irrigation channels and sluices. The men responsible were the drowners.

Hatches in the sluices were raised or lowered to direct the water into channels that might be raised in banks above the level of the meadow to carry it further before feeding into lesser channels. The channels would have to be dug clear and their banks repaired where cows had trodden them down,

ABOVE
The interior of St Andrew's Church, West Stafford, probably where Tess and Angel Clare were married. The nave and most of its wooden fittings date from 1640 with some 16th-century windows, though the chancel is modern. The candelabra and sconces on the screen were presented in 1713.

LEFT
Bere Regis Church, where Tess discovers the Turberville tombs and memorials. Hardy has her family camping with their furniture under the stained glass window on the right which is embellished with Turberville shields.

especially in preparation for the winter irrigation. In winter the aim would be to spread the rich alluvial deposit of silt brought down by the river, leaving the water to lie for a week or two perhaps; in summer the aim would be to keep it just sufficiently wet to keep the grass watered so that the cattle could feed. The drowner had to continually monitor and respond to the state of the river, whose flow would result from earlier rainfall in the area of its watershed

The bridge and Woolbridge Manor at Wool. This is the 'Wellbridge Manor' where Tess and Angel pass their wedding night.

(not just from local downpours) not only ensuring the land got enough water, but opening or digging channels to drain off land that got too much.

Today, many of the sluices and channels survive, but their hatches are often removed or broken and the drowner's skills are lost.

From Angel Clare's vantage point above the valley he could look down on Bockhampton and Stinsford and across to Rainbarrow. Below, on this side of the Frome is West Stafford, a village of thatched cottages with St. Andrew's Church, which fits the description Hardy gives for the church in which Tess and Angel Clare were married. East of the village is Talbothays Lodge, the house which Hardy designed for his brother Henry, but there is no actual building that can be identified as the Talbothays at which Tess Durbyfield worked as a dairymaid. Hardy is said

to have placed it on a piece of land belonging to his father that had no farm-house. Lower Lewell Farm, further east along the road is where many people like to place it, and it would be somewhere in this locality.

Further east and closer to the river is Woodsford. The repair of Woodsford Castle by Hardy's father, a large thatched building just outside the village, set him on his first career in architecture. Young Thomas helped with some preliminary drawings and John Hicks, who was in charge, offered an apprenticeship. Parts of the 'castle', a large fortified manor house, date back to the 14th century.

There are two weirs along this stretch of the river which have both been identified as the 'Shadwater Weir' where Eustacia Vye and Damon Wildeve drown in *The Return of the Native*. Sturt's Weir, further upstream is probably the one Hardy had in mind, but the other, at Woodsford, has a deep pool which may be where Retty Priddle tries to drown herself in *Tess*.

Moreton, the next village downstream, is the burial place of T.E. Lawrence (Lawrence of Arabia) whose grave lies in the churchyard of its beautiful church whose windows have unusual engraved glass by Laurence Whistler, replacing ones blown out by a bomb in 1940. Over a footbridge across the Frome is Cloud's Hill, Lawrence's cottage – as Private T.E. Shaw he was stationed with the Tank Corps at nearby Bovington Camp, and he was killed riding his motorcycle in the local lanes.

Southward from here is bleak Winfrith Heath, now dominated by the modern Atomic Energy Establishment, but on the Frome the next is Wool (Hardy's 'Wellbridge'), much bigger than in Hardy's day because of the growth of modern housing, though many old cottages still line the little stream which feeds into the Frome leading to the church of the Holy Rood. Here, across the ancient bridge over which the spectral Turberville ghost is said to drive on Christmas Eve, is Woolbridge Manor, where Tess and Angel Clare passed their ill-fated honeymoon. To the east, though not quite so close as Hardy locates them in the novel, are the ruins of the Cistercian Bindon Abbey, with the empty stone coffin of an Abbot in which Angel lays Tess and the river at Bindon Mill where he is described as sleep-walking with her in his arms across a narrow plank above the mill race.

The Frome reaches its end at Wareham, Hardy's 'Anglebury', before entering the almost land-locked expanse of sea, now known as Poole Harbour. This was the end of the Reddleman day's journey in *The Return of the Native*, where Manston met the postman in *Desperate Remedies* and where Ethelberta stayed at the Red Lion Inn in *The Hand of Ethelberta*. Wareham was an important port long before Poole, but the building of larger ships and the silting up of the river reduced its viability. Vikings raided and overwintered here in 876 and the town is still closed in on three sides by earthwork defences raised by Alfred the Great. Hardy's friend, Hermann Lea, recounted a local legend that they had been built in an attempt to keep the cuckoo in the town. The bird always arrived on Wareham Fair Day, but did not stay, so the next year they built earth walls to shut it in. The bird came exactly when expected, but flew off, just skimming the walls' top, making one of the builders say: 'Ther' now, if we'd a-builded they walls zix inches higher he 'ould' never have a-vleed away'.

Nine Hatches Weir near Woodsford, one of the contenders for 'Shadwater Weir'.

THE DORSET COAST

One of Hardy's stories in *A Changed Man and Other Tales* is set in the west of Cornwall and the Scilly Isles 'Isles of Lyonesse', and there are south Devon settings at Exeter 'Exonbury', and Sidmouth 'Idmouth' in 'The Romantic Adventures of a Milkmaid' and in some poems. Plymouth was Emma Hardy's birthplace, it features in poems relating to her that resulted from a visit. However, it is not really until one reaches Dorset that the south coast begins to play an important part in Hardy's work, and this was, of course, the coast that he knew best. It presents a considerable variety of spectacular rock formations, coves, sandy beaches, dramatic cliffs, pebble strands, harbours and seaside resorts.

Westward, just inside the county, is Lyme Regis, its literary connections more with Jane Austen's *Persuasion* and John Fowle's *A French Lieutenant's Woman* than with Hardy, but it is an important place in Dorset history.

During the Civil War, Lyme supported the Parliamentarians and withstood siege by King Charles's forces when most of the country was taken by the Royalists, and it was on the beach west of the Cobb that the Duke of Monmouth, Charles II's illegitimate son, landed in 1685, to lead his attempt to wrest the throne from his uncle James II.

It was in the Blue Lias cliffs at Lyme that 11-year-old Mary Anning discovered the fossil of a nearly complete ichthyosaur. Local cliffs still produce fossils, especially the Black Ven to the east. Collecting them from the cliff should be left to professional geologists, for landslips here are frequent and can be dangerous.

Fossils are sometimes washed up onto the beach eastwards at the mouth of the River Char. The little town of Charmouth, is a short distance inland, hardly more than one street climbing the west side of the valley.

Beyond Charmouth are the cliffs of Stonebarrow (also fossil-bearing and dangerous) and then Golden Cap, the highest point of all the southern coast of England, then Seatown and Eype, little villages with shingle beaches, followed by West Bay, previously of commercial importance as Bridport Harbour. Bridport town is inland, ringed by small hills, already thriving when the Domesday book was written in 1086 and it has been famous for rope-making since the 13th century. West Bay and

The east cliffs at West Bay, flanking the port of Bridport, 'Port Bredy', are clearly stratified with bands of stone and yellow sand and are rich in fossils.

Bridport 'Port Bredy' are the setting for 'Fellow Townsmen' in Hardy's *Wessex Tales*.

After the pretty village of Burton Bradstock, Chesil Beach begins, continuing for 25km (16 miles) to Portland. At first it runs beneath cliffs but more than half its length earns it its alternative name of Chesil Bank, a high ridge of pebbles that separates the sea from a placid lagoon known as the Fleet. At the Portland end the ridge bank is 60 m (200ft) wide and at its highest rises to 12 m (40ft) high The pebbles are larger at the Portland end, grading smaller to the north; it is claimed that a local, cast

up here at night or in a fog, could tell how far along he was by the pebble size.

On the seaward side the incoming and backward tugging waves move the stones in a constant susurration, even on the calmest day; but even when the seas are strong the Fleet usually stays peaceful and protected. South-westerly gales sweeping up from the Atlantic can drive a sailing ship onto the beach and crashing waves dash it upon the pebbles. West Bay, at the southern end, near Portland, not the place already mentioned, has seen many shipwrecks. In *The Well-Beloved* and *The Dynasts* Hardy appropriately calls it Deadman's

Looking down the Fleet and Chesil Beach from above Abbotsbury, with St. Katherine's Chapel in the middle distance.

RIGHT
The statue of George III, erected
by a grateful populace in 1809.
The statue and the rest of the
sculpture are of painted Coade
stone, a water and weatherproof
artificial stone which has never
been equalled. Invented by
Dorsetwoman Eleanor Coade in
the 1770s, it made moulded
figures and decorations possible
and was widely used for statues,
urns, architectural embellishments
and garden ornaments until 1840,
when the Coade London factory
closed down and the secret of its
composition lost.

Bay. In November 1795, seven naval
vessels were wrecked here, with a loss
of 200 or more lives: in 1824 two
West-Indiamen were lost here with all
hands and a sloop was flung right
across the bank, which was later
refloated in the Fleet.

It was not only mariners who were
drowned in that storm in November
1824, a storm which Hardy mentions in
The Well-Beloved. The gale, combined
with a freak tide, breached the bank
and swept the sea right across to the
Fleet. At about four in the morning a
great wave struck Fleet village on the
inner bank, destroying some of its
houses and drowning two dozen people
in their beds.

At the western end of the Fleet is the
Abbotsbury Swannery, where the
waters rose by more than 7 m (22 ft) in
that 1824 inundation. The colony of

mute swans was established there by monks of the local abbey in the 14th century to provide birds for their table. It is the largest swannery in England, with 400-800 swans there in the breeding season. Eelgrass, *Zostera marina*, growing in the brackish water, is a favourite food of swans.

Though originally a fishing village, Abbotsbury and the remains of its Benedictine abbey are set some way back from the sea. This is Hardy's Abbotsea and Abbot's Beach, set in a green valley and sheltered by a hill between it and the sea. Its 17th- and 18th-century thatched cottages are built of local stone, much of it taken from the old monastic buildings. Little remains of the abbey itself: part of the gateway, the chapel of St. Catherine stands isolated on the hill above, which was probably preserved because it was useful to mariners as a landmark from the sea, and there is the great tithe barn, built to house the tithe or one tenth of the produce collected from the lands within its jurisdiction.

The barn, the main structure of which dates from about 1400, is 83 m (272) ft long and probably the largest in Britain; though sometimes suggested as the inspiration for the sheep-shearing scene in *Far from the Madding Crowd*, Hardy identified that at Cerne Abbas as 'typifying' the location. The roof dates from the 17th century.

The Isle of Portland is Hardy's 'Isle of Slingers' and the main setting for *The Well-Beloved*. It is not quite a real island, but the Chesil Beach is its only natural connection to the mainland. It has been quarried for its stone since the 17th century – Christopher Wren used it for St. Paul's Cathedral in London, and the almost treeless peninsular is scarred with stone-workings. There are two castles here: one dating from Norman times, Hardy's 'Red King Castle', above

Church Ope Cove and Portland Castle, built in 1520, which is now within the modern naval base and weapons research establishment, for which the massive harbour and breakwater to the east of Chesil Bank were built between 1849-72. A 17th-century house which Hardy makes Avice Caro's in *The Well-Beloved* now forms part of Portland museum.

The southernmost tip of the island, Portland Bill, is a promontory reaching out into the channel on which Hardy imagines himself in the poem 'The Souls of the Slain' as the spirits of soldiers killed in Africa come home overhead. Here are three lighthouses, the earliest of which, built in 1788, is now a bird observatory, and the latest, dating from 1905, is still in use.

Beyond the Chesil Beach and Portland is the resort of Weymouth,

OPPOSITE
The tithe barn at Abbotsbury, often suggested as the model for the Great Barn in *Far from the Madding Crowd*. The Abbey was founded by a member of the court of King Canute at the beginning of the 11th century. The monks originally came from Cerne Abbas where there is another barn which Hardy identified as the original barn for the sheep-shearing celebration.

BELOW
Weymouth beach. When Hardy worked in Weymouth, which appears in several of his works as 'Budmouth', he would often swim in the mornings and go rowing in the bay in the evening.

Hardy's 'Budmouth', formed from two separate towns developed in the 13th century on either side of the mouth of the River Wey, though there was a Roman port, possibly on Radipole Lake, upsteam of the modern harbour, when coastline and sea levels were different from today. Hardy visited Weymouth in his boyhood and often later, living here when working for Crickmay. As Budmouth, it appears in many of his poems and novels, especially *Desperate Remedies* and *The Trumpet Major*.

Melcombe Regis, to the north, which is said to be where the Black Death, the bubonic plague which decimated Europe, was brought ashore in 1348, became one with the town of Weymouth in 1571.

Though this is still a busy harbour with cross-channel ferries sailing to Cherbourg, its importance as a port declined in the 18th century: but Weymouth became fashionable as a resort. In 1780 the Duke of Gloucester built a house (now part of the hotel that bears his name) and encouraged his brother George III to visit. From 1789 to 1805 the king put Weymouth firmly on the map. Fashionable society was pleased to find an extensive, gently sloping sandy beach down which their bathing machines would carry them to the water. These were huts on wheels, drawn by horses, from which the bather stepped down into the sea. When King George was in residence the town paid a band to play 'God Save the King' whenever he went bathing. The town's gratitude for royal patronage is acknowledged in a statue erected by its 'grateful inhabitants' in 1809 to celebrate the 50th year of his reign.

Weymouth grew rapidly, with many attractive late 18th- and early 19th-century terraces, curving around the sandy bay, and the coming of the railway brought further expansion and a widening range of holidaymakers. The terraces along the esplanade are little changed from Hardy's time and donkey rides upon the sands are as popular as ever.

In a wooded valley, partway up the road from Weymouth to Dorchester, is the little village of Upwey. A spring there known as the Wishing Well has attracted tourists as long as Weymouth itself. A little down the stream which flows from it is Upwey Mill. Hardy knew the people who lived there and it is almost certainly the place described in *The Trumpet Major* where Bob Loveday escapes the press gang by way of the sack hoist.

East of Weymouth, past Osmington Mills and Ringstead Bay, where the action of oxidizing iron pyrites set the shale alight in 1826 giving one section the name of Burning Cliff, the cliffs become chalk, reaching a high point at White Nothe Cliff. Then comes Durdle

BELOW

As well as raising a monument in the town, the grateful people of Weymouth had this equestrian figure of George III cut into the chalk of the downs near Osmington and Sutton Poyntz to the north-west in 1815. It is visible from the town. In *The Trumpet Major*, John Loveday takes Anne Garland to see 'forty navvies at work' making the figure.

LEFT
Poxwell Manor, a little inland from Osmington, is the original for 'Oxwell', the home of the Derrimans in *The Trumpet Major*, though now carefully restored and no longer in the dilapidated state that Hardy described it. The house dates from about 1600, the gatehouse and enclosing wall from 1634.

Door, a huge arch of stone which the sea has cut through a promontory of rock strata which has been forced nearly vertical. This is a stretch of coast where the twisting and bending of the strata and the effects of erosion are clearly to be seen at Lulworth Cove, where the sea has broken through the outer barrier of hard limestone rock and scoured an oval amphitheatre in the softer Wealden clays and chalk behind.

In *Desperate Remedies,* Hardy describes a steamboat excursion from Weymouth to Lulworth Cove, similar to one he made with his sister in 1868. It is here that the bodies of Stephen Hardcombe and his cousin's wife are cast up in *A Few Crusted Characters* and it appears in poems and in *The Dynasts*: but it is probably most remembered by Hardy readers as the place from which Sergeant Troy sets out to swim, his disappearance leading to the belief that he has drowned.

To the east of Lulworth is an area known as the 'Fossil Forest', now protected as a geological reserve, where rings in the rock are the fossil remains of algae growths which surrounded the trunks of tree which once filled the centre hole. Though none can now be seen *in situ,* the County Museum has an example where the fossilized wood survives.

Chalk cliffs circle Worbarrow Bay before the limestone emerges from the sea again in a jagged line of rocks. Kimmeridge Bay, where the father of Eliza Nicholls, Hardy's first fiancée,

BELOW
Durdle Door, a great natural arch cut by the sea in stratas of rock which have been folded into a near vertical position.

The Town Hall, Swanage. Although the building was designed by Hardy's one-time employer, G.R. Crickmay in 1872, the whole centre section of this façade is two centuries older, having been brought from London in 1883 where it was originally part of the Mercers' Hall in Cheapside in the City of London.

had been a coastguard, has cliffs on each side of dark shale. You can see a Roman table support made from it in Dorset Museum. It can be worked like wood, turned on a lathe when newly quarried, and polishes to a shiny black.

This coast must already be considered part of the Isle of Purbeck. It is not a true island, though it is almost cut off by rivers from the rest of Dorset. It has been quarried for its limestone and for Purbeck marble. This marble, formed from freshwater molluscs can be cut and highly polished. It is a decorative rather than building stone, used by the Romans for fine dressings and as inscribed slabs. It weathers badly so is not suitable for exterior surfaces. Extensively quarried in the middle ages, it all appears to have been worked out. Clay has also been extensively mined and quarried here. Purbeck is the setting for *The Hand of Ethelberta*.

The limestone cliffs continue to

Durlston Head, where the coast turns north to Swanage. Chalk does not reappear until the other side of Swanage Bay with the Foreland and Old Harry Rocks.

This was an area Hardy knew well for he lived in Swanage and liked to walk with Emma on cliffs like Durlston Head with the waves pounding down below. Swanage, the 'Knollsea' of *The Hand of Ethelberta*, was a small fishing port, also used for shipping stone when William Pitt (whose house at Encombe is the 'Enckworth' of the novel, though altered) tried to turn it into a resort like Weymouth. But it had grown little when the Hardys took West End cottage (Captain Flower's in the book) and only really developed after the arrival of the railways in 1885. There are 18th century houses on Church Hill by the pretty mill pond but more intriguing is the Town Hall, designed by Hardy's employer Crickmay.

Beyond Swanage the chalk returns at Ballard Down leading to the Foreland with the Old Harry Rocks pointing across to the Isle of Wight (Hardy's 'The Island') where the strata continues in the row of vertical rocks known as the Needles. There has been change here, too, since Hardy's time. Two of the chalk stacks were known as Old Harry and Old Harry's Wife but the latter was destroyed by the sea in 1896. Northward, Studland reaches out almost to meet the sandbanks which extend from Bournemouth to encompass Poole Harbour.

Studland, part of which is a nature reserve, still preserves wild heath as it was long before the times in which Hardy's books are set, and is an important area for heath and wetland plants and animals.

At the heart of the Isle of Purbeck, set in a gap in the spine of the chalk ridge of the Purbeck Hills, is the village

of Corfe Castle (Hardy's 'Corvsgate'), named for the fortress beneath which it clusters. It was a centre for working Purbeck marble. Limestone quarrying continued when the marble was worked out and the 'Ancient Society of Purbeck Marblers and Stone Cutters' still survives.

The castle dates back to the Saxon period and remains still survive from the Norman castle begun in 1080 with a square keep surrounded by a bailey. Royal apartments and further fortifications were added by King John and it was completed in its present form by Edward I. At the time of Elizabeth I it ceased being a royal castle but during the Civil War was in Royalist hands. It withstood a siege by the Parliamentary forces in 1643 by Lady Bankes, her maids and a garrison of five men, they being the sole inhabitants at the time. Parliament tried again in 1646 and that time succeeded by treachery in entering the castle in the guise of reinforcements. After that, they

blew it up, leaving the ruin as we see it today.

Poole Harbour is said to be the world's largest natural harbour, after Sydney, Australia. Its much indented coastline totals some 160 km (100 miles) but its entrance is less than 800m (½ mile). There are numerous islands of which the largest is Brownsea. To the

north of the island is an important nature reserve.

Poole itself, the 'Havenpool' of the story 'To Please his Wife', is on the eastern side. It began to develop as an important port in the 13th century, replacing Wareham where shallower water offered less draught for shipping. (Earlier there had been a Roman port to the north, near Hamworthy.) This was a prosperous centre for the triangular trade with Newfoundland and the Mediterranean in the 17th and 18th centuries and is now a major yachting centre. The old town, which still has some attractive Georgian houses, has been largely swamped by more modern development – more than half the old buildings were demolished for re-development in the three decades after World War Two. It is now contiguous with Bournemouth and together they spread out over much of the old heathland.

Hardy's 'Sandbourne', actually Bournemouth, was transformed from natural heath to a bustling resort in less than 50 years. The first house was built in 1811 in a peaceful valley near the mouth of the little River Bourne as a summer residence for Lewis Tregonwell. Then, in 1837, Sir George Tapps-Gervis planned to develop a resort and some villas and a hotel were built: but growth was very slow. When Hardy was born there were only a couple of dozen buildings here and at

The Old Harry Rocks off the Foreland, Swanage.

LEFT
The Custom House at Poole,
rebuilt after a fire in 1813.
It reproduces the architecture
of the earlier late 18th-century
building.

BELOW
Godlingston Heath, near Studland,
looking across Poole Harbour
to Bournemouth.

the 1851 census the population was 695. Even when the railway arrived in 1870 it was still only 2000. Thereafter, the town expanded and by 1900 had a population of 60,000 – now it is more than 140,000.

Much of the attractive character of Bournemouth comes from the wooded valleys, locally known as chines, which cut through the cliffs. Their firs are not indigenous but were introduced in the 19th century in the first formal gardens. Firtop Villa in *The Hand of Ethelberta* would have been one of the new houses among the pines when Bournemouth had its first wooden pier built in 1861. By the time of Tess, the railway had arrived and the town was already growing rapidly.

Like large parts of the Dorset coast the cliffs are unstable, so houses were set back from the sea and there is no built up parade as in Weymouth. Below the cliffs, stretching continuously from Poole to Hengistbury Head, is 16 km (10 miles) of sandy beach. The urban area extends further, except for the still wild headland, east to Christchurch, and to the north it has absorbed several small villages. Bournemouth and Christchurch were part of Hampshire until 1972. When they became part of Dorset they added another 20 per cent to its population!

Beyond Christchurch, Tess and Angel Clare flee into the New Forest and Hardy often came here himself for picnics. Though some other Hampshire places provide him with locations along the coast, he uses only Southsea, his 'Solentsea' in *An Imaginative Woman*, which also makes allusions to the Isle of Wight (where Henchard meets Lucetta in *The Mayor of Casterbridge*). Though there are references elsewhere to Southampton and to Portsmouth, where Nelson's flagship, H.M.S. Victory can still be seen, he sets no stories there. This is the end of Hardy's Wessex coast.

The Beach at Bournemouth.